Arnold, Sandra Martin

92   Alicia Alonso:first lady of th
Alonso e ballet
218046

DATE DUE			

GAYLORD M2

ALICIA ALONSO

ALICIA ALONSO

First Lady of the Ballet

SANDRA MARTÍN ARNOLD

WALKER AND COMPANY
NEW YORK

First published in the United States of America in 1993 by Walker Publishing Company, Inc.

Published simultaneously in Canada by Thomas Allen & Son Canada, Limited, Markham, Ontario

Library of Congress Cataloging-in-Publication Data
Arnold, Sandra Martín.
Alicia Alonso: first lady of the ballet / Sandra Martín Arnold.
p.   cm.
Includes bibliographical references (p.   ) and index.
Summary: A biography of the Cuban ballerina who founded her own ballet school and company, performed with the Ballet Russe, and continued to dance even after she lost her sight.
ISBN 0-8027-8242-6. —ISBN 0-8027-8243-4 (lib. bdg.)
1. Alonso, Alicia, 1921–   —Juvenile literature.   2. Ballet dancers—Cuba—Biography—Juvenile literature.   [1. Alonso, Alicia, 1921–   .   2. Ballet dancers.]   I. Title.
GV1785.A63A76   1993
792.8'028'092—dc20
[B]   93-18098
CIP
AC

Printed in the United States of America

2   4   6   8   10   9   7   5   3   1

Book designed by Shelli Rosen

Para mis padres Mario y Justa
and for Philip and Monica.

CONTENTS

ALICIA ALONSO

ONE

"I Am Standing on My Toes, on My Toes"

ALICIA LAY VERY STILL in her bed, her eyes heavily bandaged, remembering the warning of the Cuban doctors who had operated on her: "You must not cry. You must not laugh. You must not move. Your only chance to see again is to be completely still." The doctors hadn't said she would never dance again, but comments made by her family awakened that fear.

Alicia (pronounced "Uh-*lee*-shuh") was only twenty years old. Ever since she was ten years old, she had lived to dance. She didn't believe in the word *never*, so being immobilized for a year wasn't going to stop her from dancing. At least, that was what she tried to believe.

The doctors had repaired two detached retinas—separations of the membranes that line the inside of the back of the eyes. The only way Alicia's eyes could heal was if she remained completely still.

If she couldn't rehearse or even move, she would rehearse in her mind. Using the bedsheet as a stage, she performed with her fingertips. She asked her husband, who was also a ballet dancer, to correct her mistakes and tell her how to turn her fingers. As he did this, she memorized every step and turn.

Her fingers became her legs. She stretched them into a jeté, a jump from one foot to the other; lifted them into an arabesque, a position in which the dancer stands on one leg with the other extended behind; and bent them into a plié, using the joints of her fingers as if they were her knees. She worked on one ballet in particular: *Giselle*, the story of a peasant girl who falls in love with a nobleman disguised as a peasant. Alicia learned the role perfectly. She also listened to ballet music until she knew every beat and every note of all the famous compositions.

For a year and a half Alicia lay in bed, her muscles turning to flab, her body wasting away. It was torture to lie still. Alicia danced in her mind; there, she was a ballerina soaring across the stage.

When the bandages were removed, Alicia could see, but her vision was limited. Her right eye had tunnel vision: She could only see objects straight ahead; she couldn't see to the side or down or up. She also had lost some side vision in her left eye. In addition, she saw only pieces of an image, as if she were looking through a badly scratched piece of glass.

When she got out of bed for the first time after her enforced rest, she couldn't stand on her own. Her husband and her sister had to hold her up. She couldn't walk, either, and had to learn all over again. She also had to overcome her gripping fear of being unable to dance. The doctor's told her that she could walk and do simple things like cooking or reading—but not dance. Alicia thought her career had come to an end.

Alicia Ernestina de la Caridad del Cobre Martínez Hoyo was born in Havana, Cuba, on December 21, 1921, the youngest of four children born to Antonio Martínez de Arredondo and Ernestina del Hoyo y Lugo. Señor Martínez was an army veterinary surgeon educated in the United States. Señora del Hoyo de Martínez was a housewife. She spent most of her time taking care of her family, as was expected of her. Yet she had many talents. She embroidered and did lacework—acceptable artistic tasks for Cuban women in those days. Señora del Hoyo de Martínez was also interested in music. It was through her musical interest that the family joined Sociedad Pro-Arte Musical, a privately endowed cultural center for Havana's middle and upper classes.

Alicia grew up with her two brothers and her sister in a large home in Vedado, a wealthy, tree-lined section of Havana. Her godmother nicknamed her Unga—short for *húngara*, or Hungarian. Alicia's olive complexion, full mouth, and big, black eyes reminded her godmother of a Hungarian gypsy.

As a young child, Alicia enjoyed dancing to records

her mother played for her. She moved her body to the beat of the music, stamping her feet and swinging her hips. Wrapping herself in a blanket or in a piece of fabric, Alicia made up dances that kept her occupied for hours. She also enjoyed making dollhouses out of shoeboxes. Her dollhouses were so pretty and well made that her little friends asked her to make houses for their own dolls.

The Martínezes were a close-knit family, and Alicia's parents encouraged the children to share their talents. Every evening, when the entire family got together, the children were urged to sing, recite poetry, play the piano, act, or tell jokes. Alicia gave solo whistling performances for her family, who applauded her loudly when she had finished.

In 1928, the year Alicia turned seven, the family took a ten-month trip to Spain, where her father had business in Jerez de la Frontera, a town known for its sherry wine and horses. In Spain, Alicia and her sister, Cuca, took dancing lessons. They learned flamenco, *sevillanas* ("say-vee-*ah*-nahss"), and *malagueñas* ("ma-lah-*gayn*-yas")—Spanish folk dances—so that they could dance for their Spanish grandfather when they returned to Cuba. He had asked them to bring him a piece of his homeland as a present.

Alicia also learned to play the castanets, hand-held hollow pieces of wood that Spanish dancers click together between their palms and fingers. She became enthralled with the castanets and practiced until she felt she could play them in any position. Alicia wanted to continue with her dancing lessons, but it was time to return to Cuba. She would have to wait.

Alicia and her family returned to Cuba in 1929. During the time they were gone, Pro-Arte Musical had found instructors to teach drama and music—but not ballet. No one in Cuba had been trained in this form of dance, which tells a story through pantomime and formal steps and positions in a continuous, flowing movement. At that time a depression was sweeping the world. Many of the families belonging to Pro-Arte Musical had lost their money. Pro-Arte Musical thought that if they offered ballet classes, they might attract more members.

In 1931, something happened that would both solve Pro-Arte's financial bind and prove key to the development of Alicia's abilities as a dancer. Nikolai Yavorsky, a Russian ballet dancer who had found himself stranded in Mexico City after performing there with an opera troupe that folded, came to Havana to look for work. Yavorsky had left Russia in 1917, after the revolution; he fled to Yugoslavia, then went on to Paris. He had taught and performed and was just the person Pro-Arte needed to teach ballet.

Despite his experience, Yavorsky was in fact neither a good dancer nor a good teacher, but the committee that interviewed him for the job thought his knowledge of ballet was broad enough for their purposes and hired him. From such modest beginnings ballet was born in Cuba.

The parents at Pro-Arte wanted their daughters to take ballet to learn poise, grace, and good posture. Ballet would also broaden the girls' cultural education. Of course, the parents didn't want their daughters to become professional dancers, since dancing professionally was considered a vulgar and unacceptable occupation. A career on the stage would bring disgrace to a girl's family.

In spite of their misgivings, the parents also believed that ballet should be part of the education that would prepare the daughters of socially prominent families for a walk down the church aisle. At the time, girls in Cuba were not expected to attend a university or follow a career. After completing secondary school, they were supposed to get married and raise a family.

Alicia, who was ten years old, was interested in the ballet class from the time it was announced, and her mother signed her up for ballet and drama lessons. Teatro Auditorium, the large concert hall of Pro-Arte Musical, was fitted with barres, handrails that dancers use while exercising and practicing. No one had heard of practice clothes, so Alicia and her classmates danced in street clothes and tennis shoes instead of leotards and ballet slippers. But the lessons were exciting; they captured Alicia's imagination and became a fundamental part of her life.

After a few lessons she vowed to herself that she would become a dancer. Soon she lost interest in her drama class and asked her mother for permission to drop it. She wanted to take another ballet class. The drama teacher said Alicia had dramatic talent and perhaps should continue in the class. But Alicia had her way.

One day when Alicia arrived at class there was a big commotion. Someone had brought a pair of toe shoes, the special shoes female dancers use to stand on pointe, on their toes. The shoes would be given to the student they fit, so all the girls were trying them on. When Alicia's turn came, she pulled the cotton out of the toes and put the shoes on. They fit perfectly. At that moment she was the happiest person in the world, and she ran across the stage to her mother and said, "Look, I am standing on my toes, on my toes!"

From then on she carried the toe shoes with her at all times. She even took them to bed with her, putting them under her pillow. She wore them so much that her father asked her mother if Alicia was ever going to walk without ballet shoes.

When Yavorsky planned the first Pro-Arte dance recital, he didn't choose Alicia to be in it, but rehearsed a few other students and completely ignored her. Not until one day, when Alicia was in a corridor helping a friend practice for the recital, did she attract Yavorsky's attention. He decided to include her in the recital.

Alicia made her dance debut in December 1931, at the age of ten, on the stage of Pro-Arte Musical's auditorium. In a blue outfit with silver lace trim, flowers in her hair, she danced a small part as a lady of the court in the grand waltz in Act I of *The Sleeping Beauty*. (This ballet is based on the famous fairy tale with the same name.) Alicia was nervous but didn't allow her nerves to interfere with her dancing.

The enthusiasm of the performers encouraged Yavorsky to present a full version of *The Sleeping Beauty* at the end of the following year. In that performance, Alicia danced her first solo role as the Blue Bird in Act III, one of the most important roles in that ballet because of the great technical skill required. The Blue Bird spins and flutters in sparkling flight, sometimes jumping very high while arching her body backward and forward. That day, Alicia received her first review, a compliment by her teacher. "Among my pupils," he said, "are many who are doing three years' work in one. This ballet is a result of sixteen months of collective lessons. Among my top pupils are Delfina Pérez and Alicia Martínez." In the next few years, Alicia danced solo roles in many ballets choreographed, designed, and presented by Yavorsky.

It was obvious that Alicia had physical aptitudes for ballet that other students didn't have. She was very flexible and could extend her legs higher than any of the other students. Flexibility is crucial to being able to perform a wide range of movements gracefully.

One day after class, a group of mothers approached Alicia and told her it wasn't ladylike or proper to raise her leg so high when doing a step that required her to extend it and hold in the air. Alicia was hurt and felt guilty because she thought she had done something wrong. When she got home, she told her mother what had happened. Señora del Hoyo de Martínez asked Yavorsky how high a ballerina should extend her legs. Yavorsky said it depended on the girl's ability. Señora del Hoyo de Martínez told Alicia not to extend her legs very high during ballet class since the other students' mothers were watching, but during a performance she had better extend them as high as she could or she would get in trouble with her.

Alicia spent all her free time in the studio, dancing. She gave up roller skating, her favorite sport, because if she had a bad fall she could bruise her legs and would have to miss dance class. She didn't go to parties and grew apart from her friends.

In 1934, Laura Rayneri de Alonso became president of Sociedad Pro-Arte Musical. A concert pianist and society woman, she was a member of an old family and was committed to the expansion of Cuba's cultural life and to the development of ballet. During the time she was president of Pro-Arte Musical, she opened the doors to nonmembers and brought top dance companies and soloists to perform at the group's theater. Señora Rayneri even encouraged her younger son, Alberto Alonso, to join the ballet classes. He soon became a serious student.

The enrollment of young men in ballet classes gave Yavorsky new opportunities. He decided to present the ballet *Coppélia* during the 1935 season, with Alicia in the lead as Swanilda, the ballet's mischievous and rambunctious heroine, and Alberto as her partner in the role of Franz, the high-spirited young peasant who is in love with Swanilda.

Coppélia tells the love story of Franz and Swanilda. Franz is fascinated with Coppélia, a doll made by the toymaker Coppelius. Swanilda, in love with Franz and jealous of his interest in Coppélia, substitutes herself for the life-sized doll and ends up persuading him that she is the woman for him. The ballet ends with Swanilda and Franz's wedding.

Coppélia's bright and catchy melodies are among the finest ever written for dance. The ballet begins with a waltz by Swanilda; she is in full flight almost as soon as the curtain goes up. This waltz also requires extensive use of mime.

Swanilda was Alicia's first full-length role. When she practiced, she tried not only to learn the steps but also to get inside the head of her character. For the rest of her life she would approach all her roles this way.

Alicia's opening-night performance was superb. She was high-spirited and charming, she danced with lightness and speed, and she interpreted the music with great precision. She had no trouble projecting the ballet's cheerfulness, and the audience gave Alicia and Alberto a hearty applause. The young ballerina was on her way.

Two

"I Want That Girl in Every Show I Do"

UNKNOWN TO ALICIA, IN the audience was nineteen-year-old Fernando Alonso, Alberto's older brother, who was home from school in the United States. Fernando was so captivated by Alicia's performance in *Coppélia* that he decided to give up his business studies in the United States and begin taking ballet lessons in order to devote himself to a ballet career. Alicia, who at fourteen was already Havana's foremost ballet star, became Fernando's partner and one of his teachers. The two young people spent a lot of time together. It was apparent that they had fallen in love, and they began to talk about getting married.

Alicia continued taking lessons from Yavorsky, who had taught her how to appreciate music and how to follow the musical phrasing and the melody so that she could give feeling to her movements. But because his knowledge of ballet technique was limited, he could train Alicia only so far. She had been repeating the same routines and was now ready for more advanced ballet instruction. There were still no professional ballet companies in Cuba, and there was no one who could teach her more than Yavorsky.

Alicia realized that if she wanted to further her ballet career and become a professional dancer, she would have to leave Cuba. She also wanted to leave because her father still believed that women who performed on the stage were nothing better than prostitutes. She appealed to her mother, who recognized her daughter's natural talent and encouraged Alicia to pursue her dream. Alicia saw new possibilities to leave Cuba when Yavorsky took Alberto Alonso and another student to Paris to audition for the Ballet Russe de Monte Carlo, a famous ballet company. Alberto and the other student were both accepted.

Alicia shared her dream with Fernando, who made plans with her to go to New York, which they mistakenly thought was the center of the ballet world.

In reality, the center was Europe: Great Britain, France, and the Soviet Union had well-established ballet companies and schools. But exciting things *were* happening in the United States. Several major cities, among them San Francisco, Philadelphia, and Chicago, had established ballet companies. Companies such as the Ballet Russe de Monte Carlo made annual visits to the United States and were well received. George Balanchine, the Russian-born teacher and choreographer, was living in the United States. (A choreographer arranges steps and other movements into dances and puts the dances together to form the ballet.) Balanchine had helped establish a ballet school in New York, the School of American Ballet, and would soon be one of the most important figures in the dance world.

If New York was only up and coming in ballet, it was *the* place to be for modern dance, a freer form of expression than ballet. The combination of modern dance, Russian and European dancers and choreographers, and Broadway would eventually make New York the dance and ballet capital of the world.

Early in 1937, Fernando left for New York. Alicia, now sixteen years old, soon joined him. They were married soon after her arrival. By North American standards she was a child bride, but by Cuban standards she was ready for marriage. Soon Alicia became pregnant. She decided to wait until after the baby was born to resume ballet lessons, but pregnancy didn't stop her from practicing at home in the living room, which she and Fernando had converted into a studio. They created a world of make-believe, in which Alicia was a prima ballerina and Fernando was her danseur noble, the classical male dancer who enhances the performance of his ballerina partner by his modesty and noble manner.

In the spring of 1938, Alicia had a baby girl, whom they named Laurita, after Fernando's mother. Soon after, Alicia began to grow restless and began to look for a place to take lessons. She found a class in her neighborhood, at Rutgers Presbyterian Church on West Seventy-third Street. Through the Federal Dance Project, the Public Works Administration sponsored ballet classes as part of an adult recreation program. Each lesson cost twenty-five cents.

The class was taught by Enrico Zanfretta, a seventy-year-old Italian whose own dance school had closed down because of hard economic times caused by the Depression, which was still going strong. The Federal Dance Project, a relief program started by the federal government to put dancers to work, gave him the opportunity to teach again. Zanfretta had received his training in the Italian school of ballet, which stresses a different set of exercises for each day of the week. This method emphasizes a program of strict routine in practicing the five positions of the feet:

First position. Heels together, feet turned out to make a single straight line.

Second position. Feet turned out to form a straight line, heels about twelve inches apart.

Third position. Both feet turned outward as in the first position, one foot placed in front of the other, the heel of one foot touching the middle of the other foot.

Fourth position. The toe of one foot directly behind the heel of the other, feet perpendicular and one short step apart.

Fifth position. Feet touching, so that the toe of one foot reaches the heel of the other.

Students practice these positions—the basis of all steps in ballet—at the beginning of their training until they become automatic. Each position features the characteristic that distinguishes ballet from all other forms of dance: The legs are turned out from the hips at a ninety-degree angle, so that the feet form a single straight line on the floor.

Zanfretta was a talented teacher who taught without music, which was typical of the method developed in Italy, and he followed the Cecchetti system of teaching ballet. Enrico Cecchetti, an Italian, was a well-known dancer and famous teacher who taught many of the most famous dancers of the early twentieth century. His system stressed discipline, hard work, and constant repetition.

Zanfretta would sit on a chair in the middle of the room tapping out the beat with a cane. He would stand up to correct students' incorrect movements. Alicia, who was shy and had difficulty understanding Zanfretta's instructions because she understood only a few words of English, learned by observing other students rather than by listening to Zanfretta. But Zanfretta saw that she was an exceptional dancer and devoted a great deal of class time to correcting and encouraging her.

As Alicia became friends with the other students she felt more comfortable in class. Her classmates admired the ease with which she made her leg extensions and hip turnouts. Turnout gives the dancer freedom of movement in every direction.

Zanfretta helped instill in Alicia the discipline she needed as a dancer. He also taught her how to execute the standard ballet steps with remarkable clarity, and he taught her the quick footwork that was to mark her style and make her appear to be walking on air.

The world of professional ballet opened to Alicia when Fernando was accepted into the corps de ballet of the Mordkin Ballet Company for its 1937–38 tour. The corps is the group of ballet dancers that performs steps in unison and provides patterns against which the star dancers perform. The Mordkin Ballet Company had been founded, and was headed, by Mikhail Mordkin, a former premier danseur, or leading male dancer, with the Imperial Russian Ballet in the Soviet Union. He had danced with Anna Pavlova, the greatest female dancer of the early twentieth century. The Mordkin Ballet was the forerunner of the American Ballet Theatre, one of the greatest ballet troupes in the world today.

Although Alicia was not a member of the Mordkin Ballet, she rehearsed at home with Fernando, who was doing the peasant dance in Act I of *Giselle*. That was Alicia's introduction to the masterpiece of romantic ballets, which contrast real life with fantasy. They take place in pleasant rural settings, where heroes and heroines aim at, but seldom attain, happiness.

In the summer of 1938, Fernando left the Mordkin Ballet and found a job in a musical called *Three Waltzes* that was to be presented at the municipal stadium at Jones Beach, on New York's Long Island.

Alicia and Laurita often went with Fernando to rehearsals, and Alicia kept practicing the dance routines with Fernando at home. One day Marjorie Fielding, dance co-director for the musical, saw Alicia practice and asked her to give her daughter Lorie dance lessons. Fielding and her husband, Charles Barnes, the other co-director, were so taken with Alicia that they created a special dance number for her in *Three Waltzes*.

Alicia made her New York debut at the Jones Beach Amphitheater, partnered by two male dancers who twirled her through a complicated waltz with many lifts and turns. She wore a long white chiffon gown and combed her hair back with a coil at the nape to keep it away from her face. This wasn't the New York stage debut she originally had in mind, but it did mean a lot to her. It was a job, too, and working at the Jones Beach Amphitheater gave her the opportunity to find out about news of the dance world and auditions for new plays.

In the fall, Alicia and Fernando auditioned for and were accepted into the chorus of *Great Lady*, a new Broadway musical. For the audition Alicia had to tap-dance, something she had never done before. She saw some dancers practicing tap steps and asked them to teach her. "All I knew," Alicia said, "was Spanish dancing and ballet but I learned tap fast, right there. And at the audition everyone die laughing and I hear someone say 'I want that girl in every show I do. She's the end!' So I get jobs." Alicia also was one of five women slated to come in front of the curtain to sing and step and make faces during what probably was a curtain change. Her English was poor, but she managed to learn the meaning of the words she was to sing. Once she got onstage, however, instead of singing she mouthed the words and acted out their meaning. The show's producer and cast thought she was hilarious.

The musical also featured André Eglevsky, a great Russian dancer. The show gave Alicia an opportunity to learn not only from well-known dancers like him but also from promising unknowns waiting to be discovered: Nora Kaye, who would become a leading dancer with the Ballet Theatre, and Jerome Robbins, who would become one of America's greatest choreographers.

A couple of months after *Great Lady* closed, Alicia and Fernando were accepted into the chorus of *Stars in Your Eyes*, another Broadway musical. Ethel Merman and Jimmy Durante had the acting leads. Tamara Toumanova, whom Alicia had seen perform in Havana with the Ballet Russe de Monte Carlo, was the lead dancer.

In spite of the excitement Broadway offered Alicia and the experience she was gaining, she was never tempted to stop studying ballet. In fact, her experiences on Broadway made her more determined than ever to pursue a career in ballet. After *Stars in Your Eyes* closed, Alicia received a scholarship to the School of American Ballet, the first large ballet school in the United States. There, her talents were broadened by the strict discipline required by the faculty, who had been trained in Russia (or, later, the Soviet Union). The Russian dancers, often influenced, or themselves taught, by the Italian ballet master Cecchetti, have been renowned in this century for their precise, often flawless, highly expressive dancing.

Alicia dreamed of having her own ballet company one day. She and Fernando got together with other dancers from the Broadway show, choreographed their own ballets, and discussed starting a small ballet company that would tour South America. Fernando even called the embassies of the countries they wanted to visit and made appointments to tour those countries. The group of young dancers, which included Nora Kaye and Maria Karnilova, even came up with different names for the company, and they were determined to present the first "murder ballet." They believed that the whodunnit gimmick would attract support for the company.

Alicia, Fernando, and their friends dropped the idea of a ballet company when Alicia and Fernando joined American Ballet Caravan, a company that presented new ballets reflecting American history and customs. American Ballet Caravan provided a showcase for American dancers, choreographers, composers, and designers. American Ballet Caravan (originally called Ballet Caravan) was founded by Lincoln Kirstein, a dance authority, and George Balanchine, who had been trained in the Imperial Ballet Academy in St. Petersburg, Russia, before and after it changed its name to the Soviet State School of Ballet. Balanchine had served as ballet master with Les Ballets Russes de Monte Carlo, the most important and innovative ballet company of its time. (It was an ancestor of the Ballet Russe de Monte Carlo.) American Ballet Caravan was a forerunner of the New York City Ballet, now in residence at Lincoln Center in New York City.

Before going on tour with American Ballet Caravan, Alicia was offered a contract by Léonide Massine, a Russian dancer and choreographer, to be one of the prima ballerinas, or main female dancers, in his dance company, World Art, Inc. Massine wanted Alicia to perform in ballets with a Spanish theme such as *The Three-Cornered Hat* and *Capriccio Espagnol*. Although Lincoln Kirstein would have let her out of her contract with American Ballet Caravan, Alicia decided to stay with the company. She felt she needed more discipline and experience before assuming the responsibilities of being the "star dancer" that Massine wanted to make her.

Prior to going on tour with American Ballet Caravan, Alicia and Fernando had to make plans for the care of Laurita, who was a year and a half old. Since they would be touring throughout the United States, they couldn't take her with them or leave her with babysitters or friends, so they decided to ask both sets of grandparents in Cuba to take care of her. Laurita thrived with her grandparents, who doted on her. Throughout their career, whenever Alicia and Fernando couldn't take care of Laurita, they would leave her with their parents. It was hard for Alicia to be separated from her daughter, but leaving Laurita in Cuba allowed Alicia to devote herself to her career.

Kirstein wanted American Ballet Caravan to deal with American themes that reflected the history and customs of the United States, so the company served as an outlet for American choreographers, composers, and designers. Alicia now rehearsed ballets different in style and subject matter from any she knew. There were no fairy-tale characters, and the music was not the classics she was used to, by composers such as Tchaikovsky (*Swan Lake* and *The Sleeping Beauty*) and Chopin (*Les Sylphides*). There were no grand spectacles resplendent with pageantry, elaborate costumes, and specially commissioned orchestral scores. Instead, one ballet, *Filling Station*, had as its main character a gas station attendant. *Billy the Kid* featured the outlaw of the same name. These kinds of characters had been unheard-of in earlier ballets. The choreographers and composers of both works were American.

Alicia had difficulty relating to the music written for some of these ballets. She couldn't follow the unfamiliar melodies, so she came up with her own system of timing. At times she couldn't understand other members of the company very well because they spoke English so fast.

Some American customs bewildered her. She didn't understand why everyone in the company called her Alicia Alonso instead of Alicia Martínez: When a Cuban woman got married she retained her maiden name. Alicia was also advised to change her name to something North American or Russian. Many dancers believed that one of the main requirements for becoming a successful dancer was having a Russian name. Alicia refused. She was not going to forget her roots.

American Ballet Caravan's schedule was exhausting. In ten weeks the company gave thirty-five performances across the country, on college campuses and in civic auditoriums, school gyms, movie houses, and concert halls. Since the company was small, consisting of only twenty dancers, a stagehand, and two pianists, everyone had to help set up the ballets. The dancers helped the stagehand set up the scenery, the lighting equipment, and the props.

The tour was a learning experience for Alicia. Dance became her life twenty-four hours a day. She danced in *Promenade*, a one-act ballet that presents a series of short dances about people one might find in a park on a summer's day. She was one of the Graces in *Three Graces with Satyr* and a passerby in *City Portrait*, a ballet in eight scenes that sketches the life of tenement dwellers. Alicia also danced the role of a tough saloon girl (one of three) in *Billy the Kid*. By the time American Ballet Caravan returned to New York City, Alicia had moved up to dancing small solo roles.

THREE

"Truly a Classic Dancer"

AFTER AMERICAN BALLET CARAVAN finished its tour with a last performance in New York, Alicia and Fernando returned to Havana to celebrate Laurita's second birthday. Both of them were also going to dance the lead roles in *Dioné*, the first Cuban ballet to be written and produced at Pro-Arte Musical.

Dioné tells the story of the love between a young girl and a handsome prince. The ballet was written by Eduardo Sánchez de Fuentes, a Cuban composer of symphonic works and popular music, and choreographed by George Milenoff, who had taken Yavorsky's place at Pro-Arte Musical's ballet school. Although the ballet was unsuccessful, by dancing in Cuba Alicia and Fernando started a trend that would last for many years. From then on, not only did they return to Cuba every year to perform; they also brought their North American ballet friends to join them. Alicia and Fernando wanted the Cuban people to be able to enjoy good ballet.

When Alicia and Fernando returned to New York in 1940, they learned that Ballet Theatre, a company founded in 1939 by former Mordkin Ballet manager Richard Pleasant and former Mordkin ballerina Lucia Chase, was holding auditions for its second season. Alicia and Fernando had been unable to audition for Ballet Theatre's first season because they had been finishing up their appearances with American Ballet Caravan.

Ballet Theatre wanted to present not only the classic ballets but also the best of the contemporary ones. The company intended to develop American dancers, encourage American choreographers, and develop an American repertoire. To be able to accomplish its goals the company would be divided into several sections: classical ballets, English and dramatic ballets, American ballets, and modern dance. The company also included separate performing groups of Spanish dancers and African-American dancers. Ballet Theatre hired top choreographers and dancers, among them Anton Dolin, the English dancer; Antony Tudor, an English dancer and choreographer; Eugene Loring, an American dancer and choreographer; and Mikhail Fokine, the great Russian choreographer who is considered the father of modern ballet. In Fokine's work, the style of the dances, the manner of their execution, the costumes, the sets, the music—all had to be adapted to the character of the ballet. Before Fokine, the composers and set and costume designers were more concerned about what they created than whether their creations were suitable to the theme or character of the ballet.

Alicia decided to try out for the Ballet Theatre. She felt she could best learn the fundamentals of ballet, of the music, and of the movements if she became part of the corps de ballet. She was nineteen years old.

Auditions were held in New York before Antony Tudor, Eugene Loring, and Anton Dolin. The company needed only two male dancers and two female dancers, but about seventy applicants turned up to audition for the four openings. The lucky ones chosen were Jerome Robbins, John Kriza, Muriel Bentley, and Alicia Alonso.

A few months later, Fernando was also accepted into the Ballet Theatre corps. Now, not only were Alicia and Fernando together, but they would be free at the same time for visits to Cuba to see Laurita, to dance on the Cuban stage, and to give professional ballet a foothold in Cuba.

Once Alicia joined the Ballet Theatre, her day was a whirlwind of classes, rehearsals, warm-ups, and performances. Alicia felt that if she wanted to succeed and develop into a strong dancer she had to discipline herself to keep up such a busy schedule.

Alicia took two classes every day, one with Ballet Theatre and another with Alexandra Fedorova, the sister-in-law of Fokine, and her son, Leon Fokine. Fedorova was an excellent and demanding teacher who had received her ballet training at the Imperial Ballet Academy in Russia, at that time the greatest ballet school in the world. Fedorova taught Alicia how to hold her head and body, how to align the parts of her body, and how to move. She also taught her how to make one step flow into the other and how to dance with her whole body. She helped Alicia shape her style by teaching her the Russian style of ballet, which combines elements from the French school, characterized by slow, graceful, expressive dancing, with elements from the Italian school, characterized by showy technique.

In June 1940, Alicia performed with Ballet Theatre for the first time, as part of the corps in *Les Sylphides,* choreographed by Fokine. On opening night, the performance of the corps de ballet was dazzling. The camaraderie among the corps members came through in their dancing. Alicia and the others felt that they were more than just hired dancers in a company; they felt that they *were* the company. There was no rivalry among the dancers. They both praised and criticized one another. Alicia has said:

> I remember the old *corps de ballet* of Ballet Theatre. . . . We were so good and we were so proud of being Ballet Theatre dancers. I remember one day in Chicago when we were resident for a while with the opera. We were to do *Aïda* and we were going to give them the best opera ballet they ever had seen. Nora [Kaye], Marusia [Karnilova], and I went to all the kids and said, 'Okay, body makeup, everyone!' In those days they would never have thought of it. So we made them do it: dark body makeup.

We had discipline within ourselves—such discipline! I think that was the beginning of Ballet Theatre, the beauty of it. (Walter Terry, *Alicia and Her Ballet Nacional de Cuba*)

In mid-July Alicia was given a small part, one of the friends, in Antony Tudor's *Jardin aux lilas* ("Lilac Garden"), a ballet about a man and a woman about to enter into a marriage of convenience. Caroline, the bride, who loves someone else, gives a farewell party for her friends before the wedding ceremony and invites the man she really loves. She also invites, unknowingly, her fiancé's mistress. The ballet is a series of meetings and partings and interrupted confidences. At the end Caroline has to leave on the arm of her fiancé without having had the opportunity to say a final good-bye to her lover. The ballet portrays the four characters as they struggle to suppress their true feelings.

Alicia also danced the part of a swan maiden, one of four in Act II of *Swan Lake*.

In August she danced her first important role with Ballet Theatre, the part of the bird in *Peter and the Wolf*, replacing another dancer who became ill. Alicia also received her first newspaper notice as a solo dancer. John Martin, the *New York Times* dance critic, wrote: "As the bird, she showed herself to be a promising young artist with an easy technique, a fine sense of line and a great deal of youthful charm."

In the fall of 1940, Ballet Theatre went to Chicago to perform and to serve as the corps for operas. Alicia appeared in an experimental ballet-play with a rather disjointed plot, *The Great American Goof,* subtitled *A Number of Absurd and Poetic Events in the Life of the Goof.* That same season Antony Tudor chose Alicia to dance in *Goyescas,* a ballet based on drawings by the Spanish painter Francisco Goya about everyday life in eighteenth-century Spain. Alicia danced the part of a *maja,* an attractive young woman.

According to Alicia, Tudor played an important part in her career: "He taught me to tell the story of the ballet with the body instead of relying on facial expressions, to feel from the tip of my toes to the top of my head, to project feelings from the inside to the outside."

In the spring season of 1941, three leading Ballet Theatre choreographers chose Alicia to dance significant roles. She was a minor soloist in Tudor's *Gala Performance.* Loring picked Alicia over the company's soloists and stars to dance the dual role of the mother and the Mexican sweetheart in *Billy the Kid,* because he saw in Alicia the warmth and sensuous quality needed for those roles. Loring was to dance the role of Billy.

This ballet is based on the life of outlaw William H. Bonney—better known as Billy the Kid—who went west with his mother just after the Civil War and is believed to have murdered a half-dozen whites and numerous Native Americans and Mexicans before he was killed at the age of twenty-one by Sheriff Pat Garrett. The ballet focuses on Billy's wild temper, gunslinging, and romantic appeal, blaming his behavior on the fictional murder of his mother in the opening scene. Alicia was tireless during rehearsals. She *became* the characters she was dancing, taking the ballet beyond the steps and music. She tried to project honesty into her characters.

Billy the Kid opened Ballet Theatre's 1941 spring season. Critics praised Alicia's performance. They called her performance as the Mexican sweetheart "outstanding" and "unique."

That season, Alicia had her first principal role, in *Pas de quatre*. *Pas de quatre* tells the story of four great ballerinas of the nineteenth century. The original choreographers of *Pas de quatre* had had to persuade the four outstanding ballerinas of the time to dance together, since they disliked one another. The ballet included a solo for each of the dancers, as well as ensemble dancing that showed off the dancers' best qualities together.

Alicia's performance as Carlotta Grisi in *Pas de quatre* was delightful. Her turns were clean and perfect, and she moved across the stage with small steps in rapid footwork. Alicia and the other three ballerinas received seventeen curtain calls. One reviewer called Alicia's performance unforgettable.

In spite of such success, most of Alicia's family in Cuba did not know she was a professional dancer. They thought she was studying dancing. Alicia was afraid to tell them the truth because she didn't want to bring disgrace to her family. She danced with Ballet Theatre for an entire year before her father knew about it. According to Alicia he learned about it the best possible way.

Irving Penn, a well-known photographer, took pictures of Alicia for *Life* magazine. He asked her to show him the five ballet positions. Penn also asked Alicia to do some ballet steps. Since these were movement pictures, the photographer kept shooting as Alicia moved. She forgot about the pictures until they were published in *Life*. Her father saw the photos in the issue printed for Cuba. Instead of being angry he was proud and pleased that a famous photographer had chosen Alicia to be his model. He bought every issue of *Life* he could find and gave them to all his friends. That was how Señor Martínez found out about Alicia's career.

Alicia also showed her father reviews of her performances written by two influential dance critics, Walter Terry of the *New York Herald Tribune* and John Martin of the *New York Times*. Her father thought the reviews were wonderful, but he said to Fernando: "Keep an eye on her. Watch out for her. There are lots of temptations."

Although he wouldn't have wanted Alicia to be a dancer, Señor Martínez knew that dancing made her happy; he accepted his daughter's career. But he never saw Alicia perform in New York. On the night he was supposed to see her dance at the Metropolitan Opera House, he had a stroke, from which he never fully recovered. From then on Alicia sent him movies of her dancing.

Alicia's career blossomed. In March 1941, John Martin wrote in the *New York Times:* "There is Alicia Alonso, on whom this department is laying its money heavily. Unless all signs fail, here is truly a classic dancer, in the sense that Alicia Markova [one of the great ballerinas of the time] is a classic dancer. Her exquisite performance of Carlotta Grisi in Anton Dolin's *Pas de quatre* is no less than a forewarning that before long she is going to step with full grace into Grisi's most famous role of Giselle."

But before the season was over, Alicia's success came suddenly to a halt. She kept bumping into things and was having difficulty balancing for turns and estimating distances. She couldn't see her partner when he was at her side. Her spatial perception was off, and she couldn't focus normally with her right eye. First she had to turn and run in a little circle, which made lifting harder for her partner.

One night during a performance, Alicia became dizzy and saw spots before her eyes. Her doctor, who was in the audience, was summoned backstage. He told her he wanted to see her the next day in his office. After the doctor examined Alicia, he told her that her right retina was detached. She was heading toward permanent blindness and had to enter the hospital for an operation.

Before Alicia went to the hospital she danced a full program in the last performance of Ballet Theatre's spring season. She danced the pas de trois, a dance for three dancers, in *Swan Lake*. She also danced the sweetheart and the mother in *Billy the Kid* and played a minor lead dancer in another ballet.

The next day she entered Columbia Presbyterian Hospital in New York City, where a Spanish ophthalmologist practicing in New York did the delicate surgery on her right eye.

For three months Alicia lay motionless in her hospital bed. At the time, doctors thought that only complete immobilization would allow the retina to heal. Nowadays, patients who have surgery to repair a detached retina are allowed to move their legs frequently to prevent blood clots from forming in their veins.

Fernando stayed at her bedside, and many friends visited. Maria Karnilova, a close friend and fellow dancer, came almost every day to visit Alicia and read her comic books. Alicia had been so busy with her dance career that she had not formally studied English. What little she knew, she had learned from listening to others, and she knew too few words to follow a novel. But the language used in comic books was simple enough that she could follow the story.

It was difficult for Alicia to remain still in bed. She moved her feet under the blanket, pointing and stretching them without moving her body. Alicia felt she had to move her toes because she had to keep her feet alive. She was sure she was going to return to Ballet Theatre. After all, the doctor had told her she would be able to dance. Yet she was frightened at the possibility of being unable to dance again.

The hospital staff liked her and took special care of her. They called Alicia "our girl." Their support helped her work through her fear and have a comfortable recovery.

Although the operation was successful, Alicia was

left with further-reduced vision. She had now lost the side vision in her right eye, and that caused her to bump into things. The only way she could see something on her right side was if she turned her head in that direction. She also saw dark spots before her eyes; these were caused by a hemorrhage in the eye when her retina separated.

After her release from the hospital, Alicia resumed classes at the Ballet Theatre, even though the season was over. She was happy because she was dancing again, but her happiness was short-lived. She began to have the same symptoms as before and had to return to the hospital for further surgery. The retina in her right eye had become detached again. The doctors operated a second time, but the surgery was only partially successful. Alicia was advised to return to Cuba for further treatment and a lengthy stay. She was also told to rest and avoid all exercise so her eye could heal.

Alicia and Fernando returned to Cuba immediately. In Havana she went to see her family doctor, who sent her to a well-known Cuban ophthalmologist. The news he gave her shocked her: Not only did she have a detached retina in her right eye but the retina in her left eye had also separated.

Surgery on both eyes was performed immediately. Alicia also had her tonsils taken out because they were infected, and the doctor felt that any infection could affect her eyes. No one discussed her ballet career.

After the surgery, Alicia went to her mother-in-law's home to recuperate. Because the doctors hoped that if

Alicia remained immobile, the retinas would heal, she lay still in a large bedroom that was kept in complete darkness. Her daughter, Laurita, was allowed in the bedroom only three times a week. At night, weights were placed to keep her from moving her head in her sleep.

While she lay in darkness, she received the news that John Martin, the *New York Times* dance critic, had placed her on his dancers' honor roll. His choice was based on Alicia's past performance and, ironically, on her future as a dancer, which was very uncertain at this point. He singled out her role as Carlotta Grisi in *Pas de quatre*, "and in general for the rare elegance and beauty of her classic style and in her performance of even the most modest bits in other ballets."

After the bandages were removed, the only exercise Alicia was allowed was to walk with her parents' Great Dane to the ballet studio two blocks away. Alicia's doctor had told her the slightest intense motion could jar the retina loose and leave her blind forever; the strenuous activity of ballet was out of the question. But soon Alicia became restless and returned to Pro-Arte Musical. There she found a rehearsal room and began to exercise again. A year had passed since she had been near a barre. The students and staff at Pro-Arte Musical kept quiet about Alicia's visits. Little by little she exercised her arms, her legs, and her head. Sometimes, in her haste to get back in shape, she strained her legs. Then she had to tell herself to slow down or she would injure her muscles and be unable to get her body back in shape. She had to practice again and again simple movements such as bringing her hands together because her sense of space had changed.

At this time Alicia founded a theatrical group called La Silva, with Francisco Martínez, a Spanish actor. Although La Silva lasted only a short time, its existence was significant. Through the encouragement of the members of La Silva, Alicia choreographed her first ballet, *La Condesita,* based on a long Spanish poem. The ballet was produced at Pro-Arte Musical.

Alicia also joined the ballet faculty at Pro-Arte Musical. This position gave her the opportunity to continue exploring her choreographic potential. She choreographed *El Juicio de Salomón* ("The Judgment of Solomon"); *Peleas y Melisenda* ("Pelléas and Mélisande"), set to music by the French composer Claude Debussy; and *La Tinaja* ("The Earthen Jar"). Her brother-in-law, Alberto Alonso, who was taking time off from his career with the Ballet Russe, had been appointed ballet master of Pro-Arte Musical's school.

This was an exciting time at Pro-Arte Musical. The school had 150 students and a talented teaching staff that also participated in the programs presented by the school. Among the teachers were Alicia's older sister, Cuca; Fernando and Alberto Alonso; and Alberto's wife, Alexandra Denisova, a Canadian ballerina.

In 1942 Alicia became a guest artist at Pro-Arte Musical. She didn't ask her doctor's permission; she simply began to dance. She performed the pas de deux from the closing act of *The Sleeping Beauty.* She also performed in several ballets choreographed by Alberto Alonso, among them *La Hija del general* ("The Daughter of the General"), set to music by Johann Strauss, and *Concerto,* set to music by Antonio Vivaldi and Johann Sebastian Bach. Alicia kept busy with Pro-Arte Musical, but she was eager to return to Ballet Theatre in New York after being away two years.

One day when Alicia was at home, a hurricane hit Havana. With the storm raging, Alicia went outdoors to fetch her Great Dane and its newborn puppies. Suddenly the glass door of the porch shattered, throwing splinters of glass all over Alicia and hurling her to the side of the porch. The glass cut her head. Blood covered her eyes. Alicia began to scream. Fernando rushed out and found her lying on the ground. As he picked her up, he probably thought Alicia's retinas had detached again. Fortunately, she was unhurt except for the cuts and bruises.

Alicia asked her doctor if she could really return to ballet. The doctor told Alicia she could dance again if she was careful. He may have thought that if Alicia could survive a hurricane and broken glass, she could do a ballet performance. Immediately Alicia cabled Lucia Chase, the director of Ballet Theatre: "I am ready to return." Leaving Laurita with her grandparents in Cuba, Alicia once again was on her way to New York.

FOUR

"America's Finest Giselle"

WHEN ALICIA RETURNED TO New York in the
fall of 1943 to dance with Ballet Theatre again, she
found the company managed by the famous impresario
Sol Hurok, who had been brought in to help the company overcome its financial problems. As part of his
strategy, Hurok waged a campaign to attract a large
audience. He hired dancers with Russian names and offered Russian ballets since he thought Americans believed that the only good ballet and ballet dancers came
from the Soviet Union. He presented the Ballet Theatre
as a company offering the best in Russian ballet. Huge
posters listed the company's name in small lettering and
added "THE GREATEST IN RUSSIAN BALLET" in large
letters. The strategy worked. In the summer of 1943,

the Ballet Theatre gave eight sold-out performances at the Hollywood Bowl in Los Angeles.

Alicia discovered that the company had changed. Her old friends were gone. Jerome Robbins and Agnes de Mille were still with Ballet Theatre as choreographers, but their ballets took a back seat to the "Russian" program Hurok wanted to offer the public. Nevertheless, during this time Robbins began work on *Fancy Free*, set to music by Leonard Bernstein, which would become one of his best-loved works.

Ballet Theatre dancers were no longer listed as a single group headed unobtrusively by the principal dancers. Hurok gave the principal dancers star billing. Two prima ballerinas were added to the company. One was Alicia Markova, born in England as Lillian Alicia Marks, but Russian in the eyes of the public. The other was Irina Baronova, a Russian ballerina. Their partner, often Anton Dolin, was another star.

Alicia was happy to be able to learn from Alicia Markova, one of her idols. Markova had joined the original Ballets Russes de Monte Carlo when she was fifteen and also had been a student of Enrico Cecchetti, the Italian ballet master. She was famous for her interpretation of *Giselle*.

In the ballet named for her, Giselle, a young peasant maiden living in a German village, is courted by Loys, another peasant. When Giselle finds out that Loys is actually Prince Albrecht in disguise and that he is already engaged to be married, she goes mad and dies. She then turns into a Wili, a young female spirit whose

ALICIA WAS AWARDED CUBA'S HIGHEST HONOR, THE
MEDAL OF THE ORDER OF CARLOS MANUEL DE
CÉSPEDES, IN 1946. *(Dorathi Bock Pierre Dance Collection at the
Beverly Hills Public Library)*

ALICIA DANCING IN *COPPÉLIA* IN 1945, AT AGE 23.
(Dorathi Bock Pierre Dance Collection at the Beverly Hills Public Library)

COPPÉLIA AT THE GREEK THEATER. *(Dorathi Bock Pierre Dance Collection at the Beverly Hills Public Library)*

ALICIA ALONSO PERFORMING IN THE *NUTCRACKER* IN
CUBA IN THE 1950S. *(Dorathi Bock Pierre Dance Collection at the
Beverly Hills Public Library)*

PERFORMING IN *SWAN LAKE* IN THE 1950s. *(Dorathi Bock
Pierre Dance Collection at the Beverly Hills Public Library)*

ALICIA AND HER DANCE PARTNER, IGOR
YOUSKEVITCH, IN 1951. *(Dorathi Bock Pierre Dance Collection
at the Beverly Hills Public Library)*

AT HER APARTMENT IN CUBA, SEWING RIBBONS ON
HER BALLET SHOES. *(Dorathi Bock Pierre Dance Collection at the
Beverly Hills Public Library)*

ALICIA ADORNS HERSELF WITH BRACELETS MADE UP
OF MEDALS, COINS, AND SOUVENIRS. *(Dorathi Bock Pierre
Dance Collection at the Beverly Hills Public Library)*

ALICIA TAKES A BREAK DURING REHEARSAL. *(Dorathi Bock Pierre Dance Collection at the Beverly Hills Public Library)*

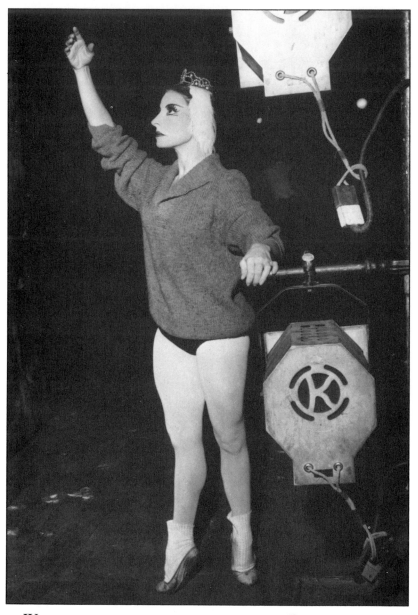

WARMING UP BEFORE A PERFORMANCE IN DECEMBER 1955. *(Dorathi Bock Pierre Dance Collection at the Beverly Hills Public Library)*

ALICIA AND FERNANDO ALONSO IN 1955. *(Dorathi Bock Pierre Dance Collection at the Beverly Hills Public Library)*

ALICIA WAITS TO GO ONSTAGE BEFORE A
PERFORMANCE. *(Dorathi Bock Pierre Dance Collection at the Beverly
Hills Public Library)*

ALICIA WORKS WITH DANCERS DURING AN AUDITION
FOR *COPPÉLIA* AT THE GREEK THEATER IN
HOLLYWOOD IN 1955. *(Dorathi Bock Pierre Dance Collection at
the Beverly Hills Public Library)*

THREE GENERATIONS TOGETHER IN 1955: ALICIA
WITH HER MOTHER AND DAUGHTER. *(Dorathi Bock Pierre
Dance Collection at the Beverly Hills Public Library)*

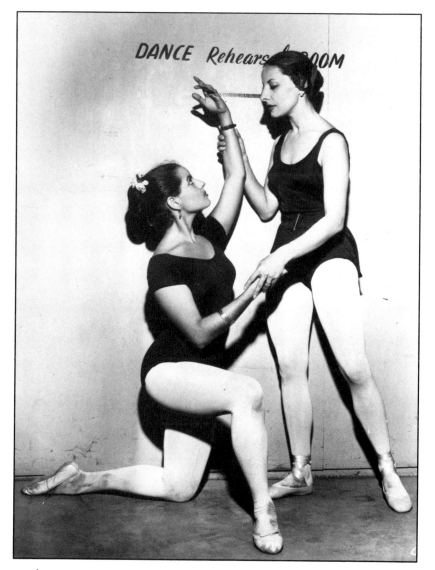

ALICIA AND HER DAUGHTER, LAURITA, IN 1955.
(Dorathi Bock Pierre Dance Collection at the Beverly Hills Public Library)

DANCING THE TITLE ROLE IN THE BALLET *CARMEN*,
1978. *(Dorathi Bock Pierre Dance Collection at the Beverly Hills Public
Library)*

WITH ESQUIVEL AND FRIENDS IN 1982. *(Dorathi Bock Pierre Dance Collection at the Beverly Hills Public Library)*

ALICIA DANCING IN 1990. *(Nan Melville)*

In 1981, DANCING WITH JORGE ESQUIVEL IN *SWAN LAKE*. *(Dorathi Bock Pierre Dance Collection at the Beverly Hills Public Library)*

ALICIA IN HER STUDIO IN 1990. *(Nan Melville)*

love was unfulfilled. In the evening the Wilis rise from their grave to haunt the forest and force men to dance until they die from exhaustion. Albrecht, who is visiting Giselle's grave, is saved from death by Giselle's love and devotion to him. No other ballet has endured as long as *Giselle*. It is the oldest ballet in continuous performance in the ballet repertoire, because it is innovative and combines great drama with dancing.

Alicia never tired of watching Markova and Dolin rehearse *Giselle*, which had been in the Ballet Theatre's repertoire since 1940. Markova had been cast in the title role since 1941. Alicia marveled at her interpretation of the role and at her easy and efficient movements.

Despite the changes at the Ballet Theatre, Alicia liked the company's new vitality and was glad to be back. She wanted to work, dance, and make up for the time she had lost in her battle against blindness.

Since Alicia had only partial sight in one eye and no peripheral vision in the other, she had to relearn how to move on an open stage. To prevent her from falling into the orchestra pit, two strong spotlights in different colors were focused on the front of the stage, a safe distance away from the edge. When Alicia danced with a partner, he would guide her with his voice and arms. When she danced alone, someone would stand in the wings with a flashlight to show her where to go. Night after night the nearly blind Alicia leaped across the stage without falling. Help or no help, her accomplishments were both a miracle and a feat to Alicia's courage, persistence, and genius.

During rehearsals she learned to feel the position for a turn instead of looking for it in a mirror. She kept her back straighter than most dancers and pulled up on her legs harder to have better balance when she turned. She also pulled up hard on her stomach muscles and gently put her feet down, lowering the heel of the supporting foot to the ground into the finishing position.

During a turn, a dancer needs to spot, or fix her eyes on an object before the turn begins and quickly snap her head around to fix her eyes on the same object again. Spotting prevents dizziness and helps time the speed of the turn. Alicia could spot only points of light, not whole objects, yet her turns were flawless and always ended where they should. People didn't know how she was able to make such flawless turns, but she seemed to have a sixth sense that helped her dance like a ballerina with normal vision.

Alicia immediately began to rehearse new roles and perform with new dancers. On opening night of the fall 1943 season she performed as a gypsy in *Capriccio Espagnol* with Jerome Robbins and as a fairy in *The Sleeping Beauty*.

Dance critics hailed her return. John Martin wrote that "the distinguishing feature of *Capriccio Espagnol* was the return to the company of Alicia Alonso. . . . It is good to have her back for she is a delightful dancer."

In early November of that season, Alicia Markova and Anton Dolin were scheduled to perform *Giselle* before a sellout audience. At the end of October, Markova was taken ill and was unable to perform. The other two soloists, Rosella Hightower and Nora Kaye, felt that they couldn't stand in because they had too little time to learn the role.

Giselle is the ballet by which a classical ballerina is judged. A dancer is not considered a great classical prima ballerina—one who has mastered the turnout, elevation, turns, and pointe work—until she has danced and been critically acclaimed in this most difficult role, which requires dance, drama, and pantomime skills of the highest order.

Giselle is technically demanding because the steps are complicated. In the first act the same steps are danced again and again as a dramatic device. For example, during her mad scene, Giselle uses some of the same steps she danced during her previous happy moments with Albrecht, except that she dances them in a horribly distorted manner that chills the audience. During the second act the dancer jumps high and lands silently, mimicking a spirit, while combining scorn and devotion to Albrecht. She also strives to achieve ethereal lightness.

The ballerina must have dramatic talent to make the story believable and meaningful. *Giselle* demands that the ballerina dance almost two completely different roles: the innocent peasant-girl-in-love of the first act and the ghostlike being of the second act, who must also express the character of the peasant girl. Using pantomime the ballerina has to show indifference, anger, happiness, grief, and madness.

Alicia had "danced" *Giselle* many times with her fingers and in her head, and she had watched Markova rehearse and dance the role so many times that she had learned all the parts. She had a tremendous desire to dance *Giselle*, for of all the classic ballets, this was her favorite.

It was in late October that, as a result of Markova's illness, Alicia Alonso got her first big break: She was asked to dance Giselle. At first Dolin hesitated in asking Alicia, because of her long absence from the company and her eye problem. When he finally asked her, Alicia's answer came from her heart, not from her mind. Alicia would dance *Giselle* even though she had never performed the role.

Dolin rehearsed with Alicia for five days. They went over the steps and movements and practiced the acting. It was hard work. Besides learning *Giselle*, Alicia was performing in two or three other ballets every night and at Sunday matinees, and she had to rehearse those roles as well.

The day before the performance, Alicia Markova sent Alicia the following note:

Dear Alicia
Here is my very first headdress I wore when I danced Giselle for the first time. It brought me luck so I am lending it to you for tomorrow evening hoping it will do the same for you. Dance beautifully.

Alicia Markova

On the night of November 2, 1943, at the Metropolitan Opera House, Alicia danced her first *Giselle* and, as an adult, her first leading role in a famous ballet. During the performance she tried to do some of the steps the way Markova did them: That was what Dolin had told her to do. But Alicia's interpretation was all her own. Her Giselle was flirtatious as well as shy, instead of fragile like Markova's. During the mad scene at the end of Act I, Alicia played Giselle with passion and angry bewilderment, while Markova had always held back her emotions.

That night Alicia gave everything she had to the role, dancing with tremendous feeling and intensity. At the end of the ballet the audience cheered. Alicia was exhausted mentally and physically. Her feet were bleeding, and she was afraid to remove her ballet shoes completely. George Schaffe, a well-known collector of ballet memorabilia, grabbed the shoes from her feet and ran away with them, saying, "For history! For history!"

That night Alicia showed she was indeed a ballet dancer in the most traditional sense: a true classic dancer. Dolin told her he was proud of her remarkable dancing. One critic said her performance was "one of the most distinguished of the entire season." Another wrote: "Miss Alonso acquitted herself with brilliance." Little did Alicia know at the time that she would achieve fame as one of the greatest Giselles of the century.

Despite Alicia's success in *Giselle*, no other starring roles came her way at the time. Markova was the star of the company, and Hurok had invested a lot of money in a publicity campaign to make her the leading ballerina of her day. She was also the highest-paid ballerina in town. So when she recuperated, she continued dancing in *Giselle* every time the company presented it in large cities. Alicia danced in small cities, when the Ballet Theatre was on tour.

She also continued doing the small solo roles assigned to her, and began taking lessons with Alexandra Fedorova again. Alicia worked hard with Fedorova. Day after day, including holidays, Alicia practiced and exercised. Sometimes she practiced alone, other times in class. Alicia was very self-disciplined. She wanted to further develop her own style, to make it unique.

In each performance, Alicia put her whole self into her part and varied her style by dancing her roles differently. Through self-discipline, persistence, and attention to detail, she found ways to make each role richer and fuller. The critics, noticing Alicia's hard work—the exactness of her leaps, the poise of her body, her fast and correct steps—praised her in their reviews. Dance critic Edwin Denby wrote that she had "perfection in the quick accuracy of leaps, in the lovely bearing of the chest, shoulder, and head, and in the exact tripping toe steps."

In 1944, Markova left the Ballet Theatre, but although Alicia wanted to dance *Giselle* and other classical roles in New York, Hurok wouldn't give her the opportunity. The stars of Ballet Theatre now were two Russian ballerinas, Tamara Toumanova and Tatiana Riabouchinska. Talented dancers like Alicia, Nora Kaye, and Rosella Hightower were not given the opportunity to develop their talent and ability further, though according to many critics such development would make the Ballet Theatre an outstanding company. Although Alicia was frustrated at being denied lead roles, she was thankful to be dancing.

Finally, in early 1945, Antony Tudor picked Alicia for the role of Ate in *Undertow*, a new ballet he had developed for Hugh Laing, the principal male dancer in all his ballets. The ballet presents the life of a young man, attempting to show why he has committed a murder. All the characters except the hero have names from Greek mythology. Ate, whose name was that of the Greek goddess of recklessness and amorality, was Alicia's most difficult role and her most impressive dramatic role to date. When she first appeared on stage the innocence and shyness portrayed by her body contrasted with her distorted and suggestive gestures. She proceeded to become the disgusting, brash, and filthy Ate through her quick movements, her posture, and her coiffure, which was curly and tangled. She was the horrid wretch who would lead all men to destruction and make their skin crawl. Dance critics raved about her performance and urged the public to go see her.

In the fall of 1945 Alicia, who was now nearly twenty-four, was finally able to dance *Giselle* again in New York with Ballet Theatre. This time Prince Albrecht was danced by André Eglevsky, who was now the company's premier danseur. Alicia's picture appeared in the newspapers announcing the forthcoming performance. Tickets sold rapidly, because she had developed a considerable following in New York, despite the publicity Hurok's favored ballerinas received.

That night at the Metropolitan Opera House, Alicia danced her own Giselle. She didn't follow Markova's style as she had done the first time she danced the role in New York. In Act I, her Giselle was a pure, warm, passionate young girl in love. In Act II, she was an elusive spirit. Once again Alicia proved herself an outstanding interpreter of classic roles through her style and her precise, well-developed ballet technique: sustained balances, high extensions, strong pointe work, fast and sharp turns, and high jumps with brilliant beats. (Beats are the tapping together of the dancer's legs while she is in the air.)

After her performance, the dance critic Edwin Denby wrote in a review that Alicia was "Markova's heir-apparent in the company" and that the performance was "young, unaffected and often very brilliant. . . ." He further commented that Alicia and André "broke through the familiar Markova-Dolin interpretation with a sincere youthful fervor and dancing. . . . You can imagine how the audience cheered. . . ." He said that elements of Alicia's technique were of "star quality."

After her performance in *Giselle*, the Ballet Theatre expanded Alicia's repertoire to include the role of a novice dancer in George Balanchine's *Waltz Academy*, a ballet in the style of the nineteenth century, set in the Paris Opera; and in his *Apollo*, a ballet concerning itself with the Greek sun god and leader of the Muses, the Greek patronesses of the arts and learning. Alicia also performed in *Graziana*, a themeless ballet that follows the musical line of Mozart's Violin Concerto No. 3. And she danced in *Le Spectre de la rose*, a ballet originally choreographed by Fokine to showcase the spectacular leaps of the Russian dancer Vaslav Nijinsky. She also danced in the Blue Bird pas de deux, considered the most brilliant dance in *The Sleeping Beauty*. It is performed by the Enchanted Princess and the Blue Bird, who compete with each other in spinning and fluttering in sparkling flight, sometimes jumping so high they seem to be suspended in midair.

When the company went on tour, Alicia danced the part of an elusive spirit in *Les Sylphides*; also performing were Dolin and Markova, who were now guest artists with the Ballet Theatre. Alicia danced with Markova in *Pas de quatre*. Together with Nora Kaye, Alicia was one of the important ballerinas with Ballet Theatre.

Now the longtime friends and onetime roommates became rivals. Each woman wanted top billing with the Ballet Theatre, and each thought she had earned the title of prima ballerina. Since a company is supposed to have only one prima ballerina, Lucia Chase, the company's director, decided to alternate billing, so that half the time the posters read "Alonso and Kaye" and the other half "Kaye and Alonso."

In 1946, with the departure of Sol Hurok, the Ballet Theatre shed its Russian image. Dancers trained in the United States were the ones now performing the leading roles. That same year, in London, the Ballet Theatre performed classical ballets, modern ballets, and two ballets choreographed by Jerome Robbins: *Fancy Free* and

Interplay. Fancy Free was the hit of the tour, and the performances were sold out. Although critics disliked the company's presentation of the classical ballets, they praised Alicia's brilliant performance and her "classical line . . . and the vital ethereal quality" she showed in the second act of *Giselle*.

In 1946, *Mademoiselle* magazine named Alicia one of the ten outstanding women of the year. A year later the Cuban government awarded her the decoration of the Order of Carlos Manuel de Céspedes, its highest civilian honor. That honor gave her the title of *Dama*, "Lady." To commemorate the event, the Cuban government issued a postage stamp with Alicia's picture.

When Igor Youskevitch joined the Ballet Theatre in 1946 as premier danseur, Alicia began her eleven-year association with him. Youskevitch, born in Russia, had left with his family after the Revolution in 1917. He had studied ballet in the Yugoslavian city of Belgrade, and in Paris. He was an elegant dancer, who had performed with the Ballet Russe de Monte Carlo for many years.

Their first performance together, the Black Swan pas de deux from *Swan Lake*, was not outstanding. Alicia ended the performance in tears, because she was still learning her role and felt she had danced poorly. Youskevitch told her not to worry because eventually she would learn the role. The Black Swan pas de deux became one of their most brilliant.

Alicia and Igor were well suited and worked hard to achieve perfection. They encouraged each other to grab opportunities onstage to show their skills as dancers.

They enjoyed their partnership and admired each other's ability. After each performance they analyzed their dancing, looking for ways to improve. During rehearsals they discussed each ballet in minute detail in order to plan each movement so they would know every step thoroughly. They were constantly refining their roles. Some critics said that when they danced, the world became wonderful. They were a magical team, and theirs was a collaboration made in heaven.

In 1947, George Balanchine, the master of ballets without stories—ballets whose essence is pure movement—created *Theme and Variations*, set to music from the final movement of Tchaikovsky's Suite for Orchestra, No. 3, in G major, expressly for the Ballet Theatre and specifically for Alicia and Igor. The ballet is reminiscent of those created during the time of the Russian imperial court, when ballets set to music by Tchaikovsky flourished. *Theme and Variations* is abstract, elaborate, complex, and technically difficult. During rehearsals Balanchine taught Alicia more about precise timing, phrasing, and the relationship between music and movement than she felt she had ever learned. Music plays a central role in the ballets created by Balanchine, so it is no wonder that she felt this way.

Balanchine constantly challenged Alicia by asking her to do complicated things. She said, "So he keeps teasing me by putting on new things—movements on top of movements—to see when I'll say, 'No, I can't.' But I never gave up." Alicia was able to learn the complicated role because of her determination, persistence, and search for new ways to learn and do things. Alicia said that in *Theme*, "my solo was in four-beat measures, but he made me step on five, and this was driving me crazy, because I felt one beat behind. But he made it work, this new kind of phrasing because you actually finish with the music." Her dancing in this ballet excelled, as if Balanchine had created a new, alluring, and scintillating personality. Along with *Giselle*, *Theme and Variations* became one of Alicia's signature pieces.

Because of her ability to dance in different roles and styles, other choreographers now began to ask Alicia to dance in their ballets. In the spring 1948 season, Alicia performed in Antony Tudor's *Shadow of the Wind* and in *Romeo and Juliet*. When Nora Kaye, who had the starring role in Agnes de Mille's *Fall River Legend*, became ill, Alicia was asked to dance the Lizzie Borden role. Alicia had to learn the fifty-minute work in two weeks, while at the same time rehearsing her other two roles.

In *Fall River Legend*, Alicia faced three challenges, all of which she overcame. The role of Lizzie Borden, a woman driven to madness and murder, required a powerful dramatic style, which Alicia achieved by delving deep into her own personality. The unfamiliar modern musical score required careful listening. And even though the dance used ballet techniques, the timing was different from that of the romantic roles in which she excelled, so she had to adapt to new circumstances.

Alicia wanted to immerse herself completely in the role. She researched the character of Lizzie Borden and the town where she became notorious for allegedly murdering her father and stepmother with an ax. She read everything she could find, and looked at pictures of the town where the murders took place. During the performance she used her body to express the dark mood of the ballet, the charged emotion, the drama. In one scene Alicia picked up an ax to chop kindling wood and then swung it with tremendous force into position in a chopping block. She split the stump in half on stage. When she brought the ax into the house, she clutched it with such fury and energy that the dancers playing Lizzie Borden's stepmother and father automatically cringed in fear. On opening night Alicia received thunderous applause.

Lizzie Borden was one of many roles that Alicia had to learn on short notice. That same season, she had to replace Nora Kaye in Anthony Tudor's *Jardin aux lilas*, which she had danced years before. The night of the performance, during her dinner hour, Alicia rehearsed her role under Tudor's coaching. Then she opened the bill dancing in a Balanchine piece. Then she rehearsed again, and finally she gave a flawless performance in the intricate role of the cool but controlled mistress in *Jardin*.

By now Alicia's dancing was powerful and energetic and so ethereal that she seemed to float above the stage. She danced many different roles in different styles. Her name began to be linked with the role of Giselle more and more. Critics were calling her "America's finest Giselle" because of her emotional range and technical assurance when dancing that role.

But in spite of the Ballet Theatre's national and international success, once again the company began having financial problems. At the end of the spring 1948 season, the dancers were discharged until further notice: The Ballet Theatre was not going to have a 1949 season. Alicia was twenty-seven years old, finally famous, and out of a job.

FIVE

Ballet Alicia Alonso

IN PREVIOUS YEARS AT the end of the Ballet Theatre's season, Alicia always returned to Cuba to perform with Pro-Arte Musical's ballet company. Guest artists from the United States joined her each year even though the company was not a professional one. Together with Maria Karnilova, André Eglevsky, Nora Kaye, and other Ballet Theatre dancers, Alicia presented full-length ballet classics.

In 1948, not only did Alicia and Fernando return to Cuba to dance, but they founded their own ballet company. They felt it was the perfect time to make their dream come true: Alicia and Fernando were both unemployed and so were their friends. They named the company Ballet Alicia Alonso. Fernando was its director, Alicia the prima ballerina and one of the instructors, and Alberto Alonso the artistic director.

Alicia invited Igor Youskevitch, Melissa Hayden, and other dancers who had been dismissed from the Ballet Theatre to join her in Havana to perform during the first season of the new ballet company. With the exception of Alicia, Fernando, and Fernando's brother Alberto, there were no Cuban professional ballet dancers in Cuba at this time.

Ballet Alicia Alonso had many promising new dancers but lacked choreographers, composers, and designers. For the new company's first season, the Ballet Theatre allowed Alicia to use its musical conductors, Max Goberman and Ben Steinberg, who became Ballet Alicia Alonso's musical directors. Pro-Arte Musical lent Ballet Alicia Alonso its sets, props, music, and toe shoes, and charged the new company a minimal fee for use of its auditorium and rehearsal halls.

A distinguished audience of government officials, high society, and business people came to Pro-Arte Musical's auditorium on October 28, 1948, to see the first performance of Ballet Alicia Alonso. The program for that night and the next two nights included *Pas de quatre*, Act II of *Swan Lake*, *Giselle*, *Peter and the Wolf*, and *Les Sylphides*. Alicia and Igor Youskevitch were the principal dancers.

The company then went on a tour of Latin America. In Caracas, Venezuela, Ballet Alicia Alonso gave several performances with great success, but its performance schedule was cut short by a revolution. Because the the-

ater had to close and couldn't sell tickets for more performances, the manager couldn't pay the dancers. There
was no money to pay the hotel bill or leave the country
until the University of Puerto Rico came to the company's rescue and paid for it to visit.

Ballet Alicia Alonso gave five performances in
Puerto Rico's capital city, San Juan, captivating the audience. In recognition of its outstanding ballet production, San Juan awarded the company the "keys to the
city," an honor given to outstanding people.

When Ballet Alicia Alonso returned to Cuba, the
American dancers left for the United States, and Alicia
invited talented Latin American dancers to join the
company. Lupe Serrano, who later became a ballerina
with the Ballet Theatre, and Nicholas Magallanes, who
later became a principal dancer with the New York City
Ballet, joined Ballet Alicia Alonso. Having dancers from
both North and South America gave Alicia's company a
professional status it wouldn't have had otherwise.

With unexpected free time because their Latin
American tour was cut short, Alicia and Fernando decided the company should tour Cuba. Traveling by bus
and staying in local hotels, Ballet Alicia Alonso gave
performances in plazas and theaters throughout the island. In many of these places the audience had never
seen a ballet.

Alicia wanted to do another Latin American tour,
but the company lacked financial resources. Then un-
expectedly, the Cuban Ministry of Education paid the
company to perform in Havana. Thirty thousand people

attended a free performance given in the field of the University of Havana's stadium. They pushed and shoved to get a place to sit down. Many more wanted to attend; when they broke apart the gates, they were allowed to get in, and rushed down the aisles to sit around the stage set up in the middle of the field. People filled every available space.

In January 1949, Alicia and the company left for an eleven-country tour of Latin America that lasted almost a year. Since there was no extra money to arrange publicity or performances in large cities, Alicia and the company often found themselves dancing in small towns in halls that were in terrible condition. In order to go from town to town giving performances, Ballet Alicia Alonso depended on ticket sales.

One time in Colombia, Alicia needed a costume for her performance in *The Dying Swan*, a solo dance created by Fokine for Anna Pavlova. Her mother, who made and repaired costumes for Ballet Alicia Alonso, cut material from the wide hem of the hotel curtains, hemmed it again, and made Alicia her outfit for that night.

In spite of the hardships, the company didn't give up. They felt like trailblazers, opening Latin America to ballet. When Alicia and Fernando ran out of money, they used their own, borrowed, and got funds from the Cuban government to keep the tour going. The company was stranded in Chile for a month because it didn't have the money to pay for the hotel. The directors and dancers were rescued by the government of Argentina, which sent a charter plane to fly them to Buenos Aires, and then paid for their lodging. Fortunately, Alicia and her company were a success in Argentina. At one performance Alicia received forty-seven curtain calls. At the farewell performance in Buenos Aires, Alicia and Ballet Alicia Alonso received a nineteen-minute ovation.

When Alicia returned to Havana, several organizations were created to give financial help to her company and to lobby the government of President Carlos Prío Socarrás to help subsidize Cuba's only professional ballet company. In order to survive financially, Alicia and the company accepted every job offer made to them. They performed everywhere they could, including variety programs on television. But they had to turn down an important booking in the United States because the company's sets were so fragile that they were a fire hazard.

In 1950, after many appeals, Ballet Alicia Alonso finally received a subsidy from the Cuban government—a sign of the company's acceptance. The Ministry of Education gave the company a monthly contribution and paid off its most serious debts.

Now a new problem arose. Many members of the company returned to their native countries after being paid, and Ballet Alicia Alonso was left with a shortage of dancers. Alicia realized that she couldn't depend on foreign dancers for the success of the company. If Ballet Alicia Alonso was going to be successful, she and Fernando had to open their own school so they could have a pool of talent available. The ballet school at Pro-Arte Musical was not interested in turning out professional dancers, and its board of directors didn't allow professional classes to be taught. People there still believed that women should study ballet but not dance professionally.

Alicia wanted students who would devote themselves to the study of ballet and wanted to become professional dancers, who were motivated to take tougher classes than those offered at Pro-Arte Musical's school. Most of all she wanted to develop a school that would train Cuban dancers.

So in 1950 she established her own ballet school. She had difficulty finding a place to hold classes because many people wouldn't rent to her: They were afraid the dancers would destroy the floors. Finally, in a renovated building in the wealthy Vedado section of Havana, Alicia opened the doors of Academia de Ballet Alicia Alonso. The school offered many scholarships to orphans and young people who had talent but could not afford tuition.

Fernando and his brother, Alberto, became the school's directors, and Cuca Martínez, Alicia's sister, was named assistant director. Alicia was to be the principal dancer and an instructor and also would be staging ballet classics and rehearsing the dancers.

The government subsidy was not enough to sustain both the company and the ballet school. To raise money, learn new techniques so she could share them with her company, and keep her name before the public, Alicia returned to New York in 1950 to dance again as one of the principal dancers of the Ballet Theatre, which had reorganized and was back in business. Fernando, who had always been with Alicia since the beginning of her career, stayed in Cuba this time.

Laurita, who was twelve years old, stayed with her father. She was used to Alicia's absences, knew her mother was different from the mothers of her friends, and didn't resent her for being away so much. Laurita understood the life of the theater and had already started to dance in some performances by Ballet Alicia Alonso.

Returning to the Ballet Theatre was difficult for Alicia. For the past two years she had been head of her own ballet company and its prima ballerina. At the Ballet Theatre she was just one of the principal dancers. Again she had to find her place in the company and had to wait her turn for leading roles. The Ballet Theatre had divided leading roles among the principal dancers who had worked together since the company reorganized in 1949: Nora Kaye, Nana Gollner, Janet Reed, Igor Youskevitch, Muriel Bentley, John Kriza, and Hugh Laing.

Although back in business, the Ballet Theatre was struggling to survive just like the Ballet Alicia Alonso. In order to be able to tour Europe, the American National Theater and Academy, ANTA, which was under the wing of the State Department's cultural division, sponsored the company's tour. In the summer of 1950, the Ballet Theatre left New York for a five-month tour of Europe. Alicia performed few leading roles during this tour but received glowing reviews of her performances. In Paris, her performance with Youskevitch in the Black Swan pas de deux in *Swan Lake* brought down the house. Critics said her Giselle captured the magic of that ballet.

A few months after the Ballet Theatre returned to New York, several of its key members, including Nora Kaye and Antony Tudor, left the company for other dance engagements. This proved to be advantageous for Alicia. Her time at the Ballet Theatre had come again. Together with Igor Youskevitch, Alicia once again became a major dancer of the Ballet Theatre. Often the ballet company signed out-of-town contracts with the stipulation that Alicia and Youskevitch were to perform. Critics said their partnership was the greatest in the dance world.

Alicia's association with Youskevitch was as perfect as it had been before. They seemed to speak to each other silently. They felt each other's passion for dance and experienced the movements of the dances in the same way. Their union was electric because they both believed they were important on stage. Youskevitch helped Alicia compensate for her impaired vision. When they danced side by side, he kept himself a little bit in front of her so that she could see him. Since Alicia couldn't focus, Youskevitch would make clicking sounds to guide Alicia when he had to lift her.

Alicia's career was reaching a crowning point. Dance critic Walter Terry of the *New York Herald Tribune* said her performance as the Swan Queen in *Swan Lake* was "a miracle of beauty in line." John Martin of the

New York Times praised her as a brilliant ballerina. Ann Barzel of the *Chicago American* said that Alicia was one of the first women of the ballet, along with Alicia Markova and Margot Fonteyn, the leading prima ballerina of England. Barzel also called Alicia "the greatest dancer currently performing before the public."

Each role, new or old, became an adventure for Alicia because she was constantly redefining and improving upon it. To prepare for the part of Juliet in *Romeo and Juliet*, she studied Botticelli's paintings to learn the carriage and line of the women he portrayed, and she incorporated what she learned into her performance. She did something similar for her part as one of the three Muses in Balanchine's *Apollo*. She looked at classical sculptures and practiced standing like one of the statues before she began practicing the role. She wanted to feel, think, and move like the people who lived during the time in which the ballets were set.

In April 1952, the Ballet Theatre scheduled four performances a day between showings of a Western movie at the Warner Theatre in New York. Sixty-four times in sixteen days Alicia danced two roles in *The Sleeping Beauty*: in the pas de sept, a dance for seven dancers, and in the Rose Adagio in Act I that expresses Princess Aurora's blossoming into womanhood. Sixty-four was twice as many times as she had danced that role in her entire career.

Alicia had become the dazzling dancer she always had wanted to be. When the Ballet Theatre returned to the Metropolitan Opera House in late 1952, she received high praise from the critics. Her performance as the heroine in *La Fille mal gardée* was described as being "enormously winning and skillful." This ballet is the story of Lisette, whose mother, a rich widow, wants her to marry the son of a vineyard owner instead of Colin, the young farmer she loves.

The Ballet Theatre's European tour in 1953 brought Alicia further recognition. Her Giselle was praised in London, where the *Daily Express* newspaper said she was "technically faultless, dramatically strong and very human." Critics in Rome described her as an "incomparable Giselle." And in Berlin there was nothing but acclaim for Alicia and Youskevitch.

In spite of her growing international reputation, Alicia still found time to dance with Ballet Alicia Alonso. Dancing with two companies made Alicia's life a series of one-night performances, theater dressing rooms, and late-night suppers. She lived out of trunks and suitcases. On the average she danced eight times a week. She had no time to think about her fragile eyesight, which had begun to deteriorate once more. She almost had another detached retina and began to develop cataracts, further reducing what little vision she had.

Alicia returned to Havana whenever she could, not only to dance there but also to spend time with Fernando and Laurita. Alicia had never wanted her daughter to be a dancer, but Laurita had insisted and got her way. Alicia and Fernando supported Laurita's decision and made her part of Ballet Alicia Alonso.

At home Alicia spent hours talking with her daughter, trying to make up for all the time she was away. She also listened to classical music and watched television. She couldn't read much and had to give up painting, a favorite pastime, because of her poor eyesight. She and Fernando prepared lessons together and choreographed new ballets. The separation from her family was difficult, but Alicia knew that the pursuit of her art demanded sacrifices.

Ballet Alicia Alonso stimulated enormous interest in dance throughout Cuba, and even seemed to awaken a new sense of nationalism on the part of the Cuban people. Cuban choreographers such as Alicia's sister, Cuca, and Alberto, her brother-in-law, became eager to create new works using music by Cuban composers, and artists created sets and designs for the Cuban company.

Even the development of the company's training included a Cuban element. In the early days, Alicia and Fernando didn't know what method they were going to use to train dancers for Ballet Alicia Alonso. Yet, they knew a ballet company was defined by its technique, style, and unique way of dancing. They analyzed different schools of technique, including the English, Soviet, and Italian. Then they chose what they considered the best from each method, integrated it with their experience, and mixed it with the unique cultural and ethnic variety of Cuba. Today this style is known as the Cuban school.

By 1954, 60 percent of Ballet Alicia Alonso's dancers were Cubans. All the members of the corps de ballet had been trained at the Academia de Ballet Alicia

Alonso. The following year, at Alicia's request, the company was renamed the Ballet de Cuba.

On May 12, 1955, the *New York Times* reported that Alicia would not be returning to the Ballet Theatre the following season. She would become prima ballerina of the Ballet Russe de Monte Carlo. Her partner, Igor Youskevitch, had joined Ballet Russe a few months before to become one of its stars and also its artistic adviser and coordinator.

Alicia had decided to leave the Ballet Theatre because she wanted to extend her performing experience and earn more money. She also knew that the Ballet de Cuba needed her personal prestige if it was to be taken seriously and gain international status. The management at the Ballet Theatre was reducing her schedule of performances. Alicia was again going to have to share star billing and performance time with Nora Kaye and Lupe Serrano, both of whom had rejoined the Ballet Theatre. Dancing with the Ballet Russe de Monte Carlo also gave Alicia time to devote to her own company. Her commitment to the Ballet Russe was only for six months a year. The rest of the time she was free to perform with the Ballet de Cuba.

The Ballet Russe was a touring company that was very popular with American audiences even though it had lost some of its prestige. It was managed by Sergei I. Denham, a Russian-American banker and businessman. Although Denham was tight with money, he offered top performers high salaries to keep the company in the public eye. He paid Alicia more than she had ever earned and granted her the privilege of traveling by plane even though the corps de ballet traveled by bus.

The Ballet Russe revolved around Alicia and Youskevitch, whom *Dance Magazine* called the "finest premier danseur noble in the world and the equally brilliant prima ballerina, Alicia Alonso."

In the spring of 1956, Alicia and Youskevitch performed in Havana with the Ballet de Cuba. They danced *Giselle*, *Swan Lake*, and *Romeo and Juliet*, which was staged by Alberto Alonso. That summer Alicia danced with the Ballet Russe and then returned to Havana to perform with the Ballet Alicia Alonso in front of an audience of six thousand.

In September the government of dictator Fulgencio Batista withdrew its subsidy for Ballet de Cuba because of Alicia's refusal to allow her company and school to become part of the Instituto Nacional de Cultura, the National Institute of Culture, which oversaw arts programs for the country.

The Batista regime had wanted to give Alicia herself just a token amount of money as a national and international figure in the world of art. Alicia wrote a letter to the Instituto Nacional de Cultura in which she said that the money being offered seemed to her like a "bribe" and she didn't want any part of it. She also wrote that the government withdrawal of support for her company was a blow to the cultural life of the people of Cuba. Alicia wanted the Ballet de Cuba to remain completely independent and not become an arm of the government.

Alicia received national support for her action. Protest rallies were held, and a Committee for the Defense of Ballet, made up of important figures in the Cuban cultural world, was formed. Alicia traveled throughout Cuba with her ballet company. After each performance she explained to the audience the offer made by the government and her answer to it.

On September 16, 1956, the student organization Federación Estudiantil Universitaria and the Committee for the Defense of Ballet held a rally at the University of Havana stadium. Alicia and Ballet de Cuba danced *Les Sylphides* and *The Dying Swan*. It was the last performance by the Ballet de Cuba until Batista was overthrown. The Ballet de Cuba now ceased to exist.

SIX

From the Ballet Russe to the Ballet Nacional de Cuba

WITH THE DISBANDMENT OF the Ballet de Cuba, Alicia, now thirty-five years old and at the height of her career, concentrated on her performances with the Ballet Russe, where she continued to develop as a dancer and was a hugely popular star. Her association with that company was not always successful, because director Sergei Denham constantly tried to save money, and his cost-cutting affected both morale and performance quality. The sets were bleak and colorless, and the apathetic corps de ballet made it difficult for Alicia and Youskevitch to elevate the general level of the company so that it was able to give breathtaking performances.

In order to avoid paying overtime, Denham had the habit of dropping the final curtain at eleven thirty P.M. whether or not the performance was over. Youskevitch almost walked out in Montreal when the curtain was dropped while a performance was still in progress. After a performance in New York was cut short, Alicia and Youskevitch decided to perform with the Ballet Russe only as special guests.

In spite of these problems 1957 was a banner year for Alicia. She was invited to stage and dance in five performances of *Coppélia* that summer at the Greek Theater in Los Angeles. The invitation gave Alicia the opportunity to show her talents as a choreographer. The cast of the ballet included both American and Cuban dancers. Among the Cuban dancers were Alicia's daughter, Laurita, now nineteen, and three young dancers from the Academia de Ballet Alicia Alonso.

Alicia's job at the Greek Theater was not easy. Not only did she have to hold auditions but she had to turn fifty dancers from different backgrounds into an unified company. The hard work was worth it. *Coppélia* was a success. Critics praised Alicia both for the production and for her performance as Swanilda, the ballet's lead female character.

In the fall of 1957, Alicia achieved something no other ballerina in the Western world had achieved: She was invited to dance as guest artist with the Bolshoi Ballet in Moscow and the Kirov Ballet in Leningrad.

At this time, since few Westerners had seen it, Soviet ballet was known only by its reputation, spread by word of mouth and through a few films. A few tourists and critics had given glowing reports about the dazzling productions of the Bolshoi and Kirov and the great artistry of Galina Ulanova, whose dancing was considered the epitome of Soviet ballet. Ulanova was prima ballerina of the Bolshoi Ballet and had been a student of one of the greatest ballet teachers of all time, Agrippina Vaganova, who had brought together all the key elements of the Russian-Soviet school of dance. Vaganova's dancers were especially known for their strong backs, which enabled them to make quick, high, soaring leaps and to maneuver themselves while airborne.

Since Cuba and the Soviet Union lacked diplomatic relations with each other, the United States had to serve as intermediary so that Alicia could visit the Soviet Union. Alicia went as a U.S. dancer of Cuban citizenship.

Alicia's success in the Soviet Union was so great that her three-week tour was extended to ten weeks. Soviet critics hailed her performances, her talent, and her training. They found her technique flawless; audiences found her captivating. The newspaper *The Voice of Riga* said her performance left the audience gasping, no mean feat considering the parade of extraordinary dancers who had crossed Russian and Soviet stages!

When Alicia wasn't dancing she went to the ballet, and took classes at the Bolshoi School together with Ulanova. Fernando accompanied Alicia and gave lessons to Soviet dancers from the Bolshoi and the Kirov, who were intrigued by Alicia's unsupported pirouettes. Fernando and Alicia taught them the technique. From the Soviets, Alicia learned to make her movements velvety smooth and further refined her ability to use her entire body to put the most into a role.

After her return to the United States, critics praised her even more than they had in the past, and audiences regarded her with awe. Other ballet dancers envied her not only for having danced in the Soviet Union, but because she had been so well accepted by the Soviet dancers and received such high praise from them. By now Alicia was the once-in-a-blue-moon ballerina able to dance any classical role, from *Coppélia*, a comic ballet, to *Giselle*, a dramatic one.

The following year, 1958, was another exciting one for Alicia. She returned to the Greek Theater to stage and dance *Giselle* with Igor Youskevitch, and made guest appearances with the American Ballet Theatre (the Ballet Theatre had changed its name in 1956), the Ballet Russe, and symphony orchestras and ballet companies in the United States and Latin America. That year *Dance Magazine* gave Alicia its highest award, the Silver Trophy. The inscription on the award read: "To Alicia Alonso for illuminating the purity of classic dance with her radiant warmth—a dazzling combination which recently brought surprise and delight to still other audiences—in Russia."

On January 1, 1959, while Alicia was performing with the Ballet Russe in Chicago, she received word that the Batista dictatorship in Cuba had been overthrown. Fidel Castro had come down from the Sierra Maestra in Oriente province and established a new government. At a press conference a few days later, Alicia said she hoped the changes in Cuba would result in a new ballet company for the world. Her words were prophetic.

Early one morning in September 1959, Fidel Castro visited Alicia and Fernando at their apartment in Havana. He knew the struggles they had had in establishing the Ballet de Cuba. He also knew that with a ballet company both of them could make a contribution to Cuba's artistic life and bring great prestige to their country. As he and an aide said good-bye to the Alonsos, Castro said to them, "I forgot to ask you how much money you need for the ballet." Fernando answered, "About a hundred thousand dollars." Castro said, "I'll give you two hundred thousand, but it had better be good ballet."

Castro supplied more than money. He gave Alicia and Fernando full authority to create a school and a ballet company. He also established ballet as a national cultural priority by signing Law 812 of the Revolutionary Government, which states: "The Ballet de Cuba will be employed in all official activities requiring ballet in its various styles, and it will lead essentially to the biggest and most exemplary diffusion of this artistic genre throughout the Republic."

Alicia's dream had come true. She was finally going to have a permanently subsidized and officially supported national ballet for her country. The Ballet Nacional de Cuba would be free of financial worries and would have artistic independence. Alicia had been given a rare opportunity to pursue and express her talents as artistic director of Cuba's new ballet company.

Right away she and Fernando gathered the former dancers and personnel of Ballet de Cuba and held auditions for the new company. These auditions were open not only to Cuban dancers but also to dancers from the United States and Latin America. Alicia hoped that the new ballet company would have free cultural interchange with other countries. The panel of judges that was to select dancers reflected Alicia's hope. The panelists included, besides Alicia and Fernando, Alexandra Danilova, who for many years had been prima ballerina with the Ballet Russe de Monte Carlo; Phyllis W. Manchester, an American dance critic; Igor Youskevitch; and two dancers from the current Ballet Russe.

At the time it seemed that Alicia would be able to continue a dual career in the United States and Cuba. More than ever before she felt she could pursue the close ties between the American Ballet Theatre and Cuba's emerging Ballet Nacional.

In the following year, 1960, Alicia continued creating links between the Ballet Nacional and the rest of the world. In March, she hosted a successful international ballet festival in Havana. Six ballet companies, including dancers from the American Ballet Theatre and from the Bolshoi Ballet, participated in the festival. The embassies of the United States, Venezuela, and Mexico gave receptions to celebrate the event.

In April, Alicia returned to New York to appear in the American Ballet Theatre's twentieth-anniversary celebration. She danced *Giselle*, the pas de deux from *Don Quixote*, and *Pas de quatre*. Little did Alicia know that these were to be her last performances in the United States.

Relations between the United States and Cuba had begun to deteriorate. The two countries were becoming bitter enemies because Cuba had begun to develop a Communist government. At the end of 1960 the United States banned all exports to Cuba except food and medical supplies. Then, in January 1961, President Dwight Eisenhower broke off diplomatic relations with Cuba.

Alicia now became a dangerous person in the eyes of the U.S. government. Although she had been invited to perform in the United States in 1961, the Department of State didn't allow her to return later that year. Some countries in Europe and South America followed suit and also denied her permission to perform.

Since the 1930s, Alicia had been part of the growth of ballet in the United States. Now she was cut off from the center of ballet in the Western world; from her friends, her audience, and her partners; and from the American Ballet Theatre, in which she had risen to stardom. At the height of her career, her name disappeared from U.S. newspapers, and Cuban newspapers stopped printing any news having to do with the United States. The two countries, although only ninety miles apart, had ceased to exist for each other. To make matters worse, in April 1961 a force of exiled Cubans, supported by the U.S. government, invaded Cuba at the Bay of Pigs in an attempt to topple the Castro government. The defeat and quick capture of the invaders made relations between the countries even worse.

Isolated from the United States and other parts of the Western world, Alicia turned her energy and expe-

rience to develop the growth of Ballet Nacional de
Cuba, a dance school, and cultural education and opportunities in the arts for every Cuban. She transformed
the house next door to Pro-Arte Musical into Ballet Nacional de Cuba headquarters. The house had belonged
to Laura Rayneri de Alonso, Fernando's mother, who
had contributed it and other property to the Castro government. Alicia turned the rooms of the house into a
rehearsal hall, classrooms, offices, and workshops.

Then she took ballet to the people. To make sure
everyone on the island had an opportunity to see ballet,
the company traveled from one end of the island to the
other, performing in factories and sugar-cane fields, in
makeshift theaters with dirt-floored stages. The dancers
did more than dance. They showed slides, lectured,
taught people how to make toe shoes, and told ballet
stories. Alicia and the other members of the company
also participated voluntarily in work brigades that har-
vested sugar cane or planted vegetables. In fact, Alicia
and the members of Ballet Nacional did everything that
ordinary people were doing in support of the new government and its leader.

It was crucial for Alicia and Fernando to get men
interested in dancing ballet. In the past, the Ballet Nacional had depended on male dancers from the United
States and other countries. The majority of Cuban men
saw ballet as something only for women. It was up to
Fernando and Alberto to interest Cuban boys in ballet.
They had to convince them that things like grands pliés
(deep knee bends) and port de bras (moving and plac-

ing the arms in a certain way) were not going to cost them their masculinity. Lectures, performances, demonstrations, and the presence of ballet dancers in work details in the fields helped some. Alicia suggested that gymnastics and acrobatics classes incorporate ballet steps and exercises so that boys could see the relationship between ballet and sports. Boys who took gymnastics and acrobatics were monitored closely for ballet potential.

Another source of male dancers was orphanages. Orphans were eager to join the ballet school because it offered a better life than the one they were living, with better housing and training for a profession. One nine-year-old orphan who took advantage of the opportunity to study ballet was Jorge Esquivel. At eighteen Jorge began to partner Alicia, and he still does.

Through Alicia's work and the new government's support, the arts became an important part of Cuban life. To make sure the best and most talented students had a place to train, construction was begun on a complex of educational buildings at the site of a former country club outside Havana. This complex was given the native name for Cuba, Cubanacán. Besides the ballet school, Cubanacán had schools of modern dance, theater, music, and painting and sculpture. Tuition was free: The government paid for everything. Students lived at the complex unless their homes were nearby.

Thanks to Alicia, ballet was made part of the school curriculum beginning in nursery school and continuing through adult education classes. Children interested in learning ballet began dancing lessons in their own community. Children who showed talent by the time they were about nine years old moved on from this general school to a more professional school near home. A first dance test came when the students were nine, a second when they were twelve. Selections were made at each school by audition. Besides dance technique, the evaluators considered students' physique, health, and physical skills. Students who reached a required level of excellence went to Cubanacán. Exceptional students went directly into Cubanacán at the age of nine, where besides dance instruction they studied academic subjects, music, and languages.

From Cubanacán, Alicia and her staff chose the best students to attend the Escuela Nacional de Ballet. The best dancers were then invited to join either the Ballet Nacional de Cuba in Havana or the Ballet de Camagüey, the second-largest ballet school and company in Cuba.

When auditions for the Ballet Nacional de Cuba and the Ballet de Camagüey were held, students were evaluated not only on dance technique but also on their intellectual capacity and dramatic aptitude. The first audition was before a board of teachers trained by Alicia and Fernando. Alicia made the final selections.

Teachers at provincial schools and at the Escuela Nacional de Ballet met every two months to attend seminars and refresher classes in historic and national dances and in ballet technique. The instructors also took psychology courses and had the opportunity to talk about methods of evaluation and discuss any problems they had in teaching. These meetings helped teachers from the provinces keep up with the latest in ballet and contribute their know-how.

Dance was also incorporated into the treatment of children with psychological problems. Psycho-ballet, Alicia's own invention, was a special system of ballet exercises, part of the total treatment plan of mentally disturbed children. In Alicia's psycho-ballet, the children began by doing simple movements, then moved on to "ballet stories" in which they played different roles. While the children acted out their own story dances, they helped themselves.

According to Alicia, when the children became involved in the story and mastered movement, they were guided into such concentration that their minds were freed of the problems that had troubled them. Alicia believed that through dance the whole body could be used to heal the mind, and that if the mind created art, then art could be used to cure the mind.

Alicia established a ballet company and ballet school that were uniquely Cuban. The Ballet Nacional de Cuba performed classic ballets, contemporary ballets, and even modern dance. Its choreographers were encouraged to create new works. And the company was integrated: Blacks, mulattoes, Asians, and whites, danced together in all types of ballets. Also, dancers of different heights and builds made up the corps de ballet. Critics have praised the corps's precision and uniformity.

In 1959, when the Ballet Nacional de Cuba had just been organized, it went on a tour of seven Latin American countries. In 1960 and 1961 it performed in the People's Republic of China, Poland, Czechoslovakia, the Soviet Union, and East Germany. From 1961 to 1964 the company remained in Cuba, working on its technique, its repertory, and its mission of taking ballet to every corner of Cuban society.

In 1964 the Ballet Nacional de Cuba broke its self-imposed hibernation and participated in the first International Ballet Competition in Varna, Bulgaria. There were contestants from eleven countries. The Cuban dancers were sensational. The world took note of their superb style and the Ballet Nacional's new look. Three Cuban dancers won medals, and Alicia's presence in the jury gave the Ballet Nacional a special distinction. Alicia's vision of a world-renowned Cuban ballet company had come true.

SEVEN

The Prima Ballerina
Who Was Blind

THROUGHOUT THE 1960s THE Ballet Nacional de Cuba and Alicia Alonso continued to garner honors. In 1966 the company was invited to perform in France, at the fourth Festival International de Danse de Paris. This was the first time in six years that the Ballet Nacional de Cuba had danced in a Western country.

Alicia and her company were even more successful in Paris than they had been in Bulgaria two years before. Alicia received the Anna Pavlova prize as best dancer, and also the Grand Prix de la Ville, the highest honor of the festival. The Ballet Nacional de Cuba won high praise.

The following year Anton Dolin invited Alicia to dance *Giselle* with Les Grands Ballets Canadiens at Expo 67 in Montreal. Friends, critics, and ballet lovers from the United States went to Montreal to see her. Seven years had now passed since some of her North American friends had last seen her onstage or talked to her.

What Alicia's North American friends did not know was that she was now almost totally blind. She could see only shadows and had lost her sense of space, which prevented her from gauging distance and depth. To guide Alicia and help her orient herself, Dolin placed bright lights in the center of the stage, at stage right, and at stage left. During the rehearsal of Act I of *Giselle,* when Alicia was required to run across the stage, she couldn't see anything even with the lights, so Dolin arranged to have Alicia run with two of the villagers in the ballet. To signal Alicia to go offstage, Dolin stood in the wings with a flashlight to guide her.

To Alicia, her blindness meant she had to work all the harder, but it was frustrating to be unable to check in the classroom mirror for her faults or correct her or her students' body line anymore. When she practiced, she impressed the steps into her consciousness so that she could rely on those images and her "inner vision" when she performed. In spite of her disability, Alicia's dancing was still great. More than ever she made every inch of her body expressive. She showed character with the turn of her head or the movement of her hand. She made her entire body express what her eyes couldn't see.

Since the early 1960s she had been compensating for her almost complete blindness. When speaking to her friends, Alicia would turn her head in the direction of their voice. If she had to walk across a room or down a flight of stairs, she did it with the help of a friend.

Alicia also had complete trust in her dance partners. That trust allowed her to leap and soar in darkness when she was onstage and able to see only a blurred space. Azari Plisetski, a Soviet dancer, was Alicia's regular partner from 1963 to 1973. He gave her the strong physical support she needed, guiding her and helping her move onstage.

In order to do multiple turns while standing on both legs, Alicia imagined she had an invisible axis about which she could turn without spotting, much the way an ice skater spins. She practiced jumps in place and memorized the stage layout before she did traveling leaps.

In spite of her many years of blindness Alicia refused to have additional surgery. She was in her late forties now, an age at which most ballerinas have either retired or are thinking about retiring. She was afraid that since she would be unable to dance for at least a year after the surgery, her dance career would then come to an end. She preferred to be blind.

Alicia's blindness didn't prevent her from continuing to garner honors. In 1968 she won a medal at the Cultural Olympics in Mexico. The following year she went on an extensive tour of the Soviet Union, Romania, Bulgaria, the Netherlands, Spain, and East Germany. While she was in the Soviet Union she served on the jury at the International Ballet Competition in Moscow.

In order to see the dancers she had to use powerful binoculars.

In 1969, while rehearsing *Giselle* for a performance in Copenhagen with a Danish company, Alicia crashed into the scenery. Luckily, she wasn't hurt, but to prevent repeated accidents and possible injury, her partner and the rest of the cast made adjustments and worked out details to ensure her safety.

At the performance Alicia's partner had to guide her to the flowers Giselle picks up. Yet critics said that her Giselle was "as overwhelming as Ulanova's" and that she was "probably the world's greatest ballerina."

That same year, because of her inability to focus her eyes, Alicia had to give up dancing the role of the Black Swan in *Swan Lake* because she could not do the multiple fouettés, the series of turns standing on one leg and whipping the other leg around in a series of turns, required in that role.

By 1972 Alicia could see only a pinpoint of light. To help her walk offstage her daughter or someone else would whisper to guide her. Yet Alicia continued to dance and tour as if nothing were wrong with her eyes. In February she staged her version of *Giselle* for the Paris Opéra and danced in five performances.

At the end of that year Alicia knew she had to make a decision: Her doctor told her that if she didn't have eye surgery she would be completely blind forever. Alicia decided to have the operation. She flew with the Ballet Nacional de Cuba to Prague, Czechoslovakia. While the company went on to East Germany, she flew to Tokyo to dance with the Tokyo Ballet Company, rejoining the Ballet Nacional in Budapest, Hungary. The Cuban company then went on to the Soviet Union and Bulgaria. Alicia flew to Barcelona, where the Spanish ophthalmologist Joaquín Barraguer secured one of Alicia's retinas in place and removed the cataracts from her eyes, using a laser technique that required her to be immobilized for only a few days.

When the bandages were removed Alicia could see better than before the surgery but was permanently blind in one eye. She felt she was ready to start her life all over again and ignored Dr. Barraguer's predictions. He had said she would not dance again because at her age—fifty-one—she would never regain her sense of balance.

The next couple of years were terrible for Alicia. Unable to dance, moody, she became involved in other things to help her through this rough time. She planned dance curricula for children, factory and field workers, and people with disabilities. She joined government committees and organizations and traveled to other countries to stage ballets.

During this time Alicia also received several awards: the Silver Sun in Mexico and the Golden Sagittarius in Italy. The University of Havana awarded her an honorary doctorate in art, the first given since the university's founding in 1728. Fidel Castro gave her the Ana Betancourt Award, given to Cuban women who have made a significant contribution to the nation.

In 1974 Alicia presented Ballet Nacional de Cuba's

version of *The Sleeping Beauty* at the Paris Opéra and traveled to Italy to receive another award. She also judged contests in the Soviet Union, France, Bulgaria, and Japan.

Alicia organized the fourth Festival of Dance in Cuba and invited Cynthia Gregory of the American Ballet Theatre to participate. Even though U.S. citizens were not allowed to go to Cuba, and one who did go was in danger of having his or her passport revoked, Gregory accepted the invitation: She felt that politics shouldn't interfere with art. She did not lose her passport. This was the first time since 1960 that an American dancer had performed in Cuba.

All this time, without telling anyone, Alicia had been exercising, learning to keep her balance, and getting adjusted to dancing with even more vision than she had had before. At a program honoring Cuban women, Alicia surprised eveyone by dancing with her partner Jorge Esquivel in *Las Mujeres*, a simple number choreographed by Alberto Méndez, one of the outstanding choreographers of the Ballet Nacional de Cuba. After a two-year absence, Alicia Alonso was back onstage.

EIGHT

"Alicia, Alicia, Alicia!"

ALICIA WORKED HARD RELEARNING the dances that had been part of her repertory. Now that she could see better she again had to learn how to keep her balance. The techniques that she had learned to move across the stage when she couldn't see didn't work as well now.

In 1975 she danced in two new ballets, *Salomé* and *Yagruma*. She also danced the principal female role of Jocasta in *Oedipus Rex*, based on the play of the same name by the ancient Greek playwright Sophocles. By the end of the year she was able to dance the title role in *Carmen*, based on the opera by the French composer Georges Bizet. Carmen is a fiery woman whose jealous lover kills her after she leaves him for another man.

Learning to dance with partial vision was not the

only change Alicia made in her life. For many years Alicia and Fernando had been having marital problems. Now they agreed to a divorce. That same year Alicia married Pedro Simón, a critic and art historian who was editor in chief of the magazine *Cuba en el ballet* ("Cuba in the Ballet"). Pedro became Alicia's guide through her social commitments, and he read for her when she had to do historical and literary research for a ballet project.

Meanwhile in the United States, Lucia Chase and Oliver Smith, the co-directors of the American Ballet Theatre, were pressing the State Department to give Alicia permission to appear at the American Ballet Theatre's thirty-fifth anniversary celebration in July 1975. The department first turned down the request but eventually granted Alicia permission to dance in the United States again.

The American Ballet Theatre sold out every seat in the Metropolitan Opera House, but not everyone received Alicia with open arms. Members of the exiled Cuban community, who had left Cuba when Fidel Castro took over because they didn't want to live under Fidel Castro's Communist government, picketed Lincoln Center. These Cuban refugees didn't want Alicia to perform. They felt she should not have stayed in Cuba and worked with Castro's government, but rather should have come to live in the United States and have worked toward toppling Castro. Alicia even received some death threats from Cuban exiles.

Security at the Metropolitan Opera House was tight. Ticket holders had to wait for an hour and a quarter in the lobby while police searched for bombs, and security guards checked handbags. Inside the auditorium, guards were stationed at either side of the stage.

But the threats and noisy demonstration could not compare with the warm reception and thunderous roar the audience gave Alicia when she appeared onstage. When she finished dancing the title role of *Giselle*, she received a twenty-minute standing ovation and twenty-three curtain calls. Shouts of "Alicia, Alicia, Alicia!" filled the large auditorium. Alicia, crying, bowed to the audience several times, filled with emotion after performing again in the country where she had had her start as a professional ballerina. Her fifteen-year exile from the North American stage had ended in triumph.

Little did she know that the first step toward a thaw in relations between the United States and Cuba had been taken. Shortly after Alicia's return to Cuba, the two countries established limited diplomatic relations. Whether Alicia's return to the United States had anything to do with the slight change, no one knows. But perhaps it did demonstrate that art goes beyond politics.

Two years later Alicia went to Charleston, South Carolina, with Jorge Esquivel to dance at Gian Carlo Menotti's Festival of Two Worlds. They danced *Canción para la extraña flor* ("Song for the Aster"), a new pas de deux created by Alberto Méndez especially for the festival. Once again the public received her with thunderous applause and cheers.

In 1978, at fifty-seven, an age when most ballerinas

have retired from dancing, Alicia came back to the United States as prima ballerina, director, and co-founder of her own ballet company. She and the Ballet Nacional performed at the Opera House of the Kennedy Center, at the Metropolitan Opera in New York, and in Los Angeles, Berkeley, Houston, San Antonio, Philadelphia, and Boston.

U.S. audiences didn't know what to expect of this Cuban ballet company composed of Cuban dancers. But with the technical and dramatic skills of its dancers, at its first North American appearance the Ballet Nacional de Cuba proved it was a world-class company. The North American dance public realized that the high praise Alicia's Ballet Nacional had received in other countries was truly justified. In every city Alicia and the Ballet Nacional visited, they were greeted with great enthusiasm.

The following year Alicia returned once again to the United States with the Ballet Nacional de Cuba to tour several cities. The mayor of Washington, D.C., declared July 2 Alicia Alonso Day in that city. And in San Francisco she received a commendation for her contribution to art and culture in North America. The Kennedy Center made her a member of its Artistic Committee and honored her for her contribution to North American culture. Two years later, Alicia visited the United States again.

In 1980 Alicia traveled to Paris to participate in an international ballet gala organized in her honor by UNESCO, the United Nations Educational, Scientific, and Cultural Organization. She became the first dancer to be singled out by UNESCO for her role in the development and promotion of art in the world.

When the University of Texas organized a jubilee in honor of Igor Youskevitch, who in 1982 was retiring as head of its dance department, the university managed to get permission from the State Department and the Cuban government to have Alicia participate in the festivities. Dancers from all over the world had come to honor the man who had been Alicia's first regular partner and with whom she had formed one of the greatest, most popular teams in ballet.

The day of the performance Alicia danced with Jorge Esquivel in the White Swan pas de deux from *Swan Lake*. Then a surprise was announced. A giant movie screen came down in front of the stage, and on it played a home movie made by Tina, Igor's wife. The movie showed *Giselle* at the Hollywood Bowl in 1945, with Igor and Alicia doing the pas de deux from the second act. Since the film was silent, the theater orchestra played soft music. Suddenly the image on the screen froze. All the lights came up slowly on Alicia and Igor, who were standing in the same pose and wearing the same costumes as in the film.

The audience gasped when they saw Alicia and Igor together again. The magic the two had as partners was still there. They danced delicately and with tenderness. When they finished, Alicia clung to Igor's hand and moved forward for bows. Then she stepped back and bowed to him. There was complete silence in the audience. The silence broke, and the wild noise of applause filled the theater as Igor helped Alicia get up from her bow.

Today Alicia Alonso continues to excite the world of ballet. Although in her seventies, she still performs — an unheard-of age for a classical ballerina to be dancing. She doesn't dance full-length ballets often, but she performs excerpts from *Swan Lake* and *Giselle.*

Alicia practices for an hour and a half every day under the direction of her daughter, Laurita. At the ballet barre, she works at keeping her legs flexible. She also practices the various movements of a ballerina's repertoire, including leaps, which are not easy to do because of her limited vision, and batterie, beating the legs together. She also choreographs and teaches special classes to the principal dancers of the Ballet Nacional de Cuba.

Nothing stopped Alicia from becoming one of the world's great ballerinas and one of the greatest interpreters of *Giselle* in this century. She defied cultural tradition to pursue her dream of becoming a ballerina. Age has not stopped her from dancing. She has proven that for a dancer, poor vision or blindness may make things harder, but it doesn't make them impossible.

As director, co-founder, and prima ballerina of the Ballet Nacional de Cuba, Alicia has guided and inspired a generation of Cuban dancers. She represents a dancer's ability to affect her art. Alicia Alonso has carved out a unique position in Cuban culture and in international ballet.

BIBLIOGRAPHY

Anderson, Jack. *Ballet and Modern Dance: A Concise History.* 2nd ed. Pennington, N.J.: Dance Horizons/Princeton Book Company, 1986.

Arnold, Eve. *Misha and Company: Behind the Scenes with American Ballet Theatre.* New York: Bantam, 1988.

Balanchine, George, and Francis Mason. *Complete Stories of the Great Ballets.* New York: Doubleday, 1965.

———. *101 Stories of the Great Ballets.* New York: Doubleday, 1975.

Ballenbera, Birdie. *Looking at Ballet.* New York: Marshall Cavendish, 1990.

Baquero, Joaquín. *Alicia Alonso.* Havana: Editorial Letras Cubanas, 1984.

Bazarova, Nadezhda, and Varvara Mey. *Alphabet of Classical*

Dance. Pennington, N.J.: Dance Horizons/Princeton Book Company, 1987.

Beaumont, Cyril W. *The Ballet Called Giselle.* Pennington, N.J.: Dance Horizons/Princeton Book Company, 1987.

Berger, Gilda. *Magic Slippers: Stories from the Ballet.* New York: Doubleday, 1990.

Bremser, Martha, ed. *International Dictionary of Ballet.* Detroit: St. James Press, 1992.

Chujoy, Anatole, and P. W. Manchester. *The Dance Encyclopedia.* New York: Simon & Schuster, 1967.

De Gamez, Tana. *Alicia Alonso at Home and Abroad.* New York: Citadel Press, 1971.

De Mille, Agnes. *Dance to The Piper.* Boston: Little, Brown, 1952.

―――. *Portrait Gallery.* Boston: Houghton Mifflin, 1990.

Denby, Edwin. *Looking at the Dance.* New York: Horizon Press, 1968.

Ehrmann, Hans. "Ballet Nacional de Cuba." *Dance Magazine,* November 1991, pp. 88–90.

Fonteyn, Margot. *Pavlova: Portrait of a Dancer.* New York: Viking, 1984.

Giselle: Gala Homenaje. Havana: Ministerio de Cultura, 1978.

Haskell, Arnold. *Balletomania: Then and Now.* New York: Knopf, 1977.

―――. *How to Enjoy Ballet.* New York: Morrow, 1951.

Horosko, Marian. "Pirouettes Placed and Paced." *Dance Magazine,* September 1989.

Kuklin, Susan. *Reaching for Dreams: A Ballet from Rehearsal to Opening Night.* New York: Lothrop, 1987.

Martin, John. *John Martin's Book of the Dance.* New York: Tudor Publishing, 1963.

Maynard, Olga. *The American Ballet.* Philadelphia: Macrae Smith, 1959.

Morris, Ann. *On Their Toes: Young Dancers at a Russian Ballet School.* New York: Atheneum, 1991.

Newman, Barbara. *Striking a Balance: Dancers Talk About Dancing.* Boston: Houghton Mifflin, 1982.

Ostlere, Hilary. "Deep Waters: Caught in the Undertow." *Dance Magazine,* January 1992, pp. 52–55.

Pozharskaya, Militsa, and Tatiana Volodina. *The Art of the Ballets Russes: The Russian Seasons in Paris.* New York: Abbeville, 1991.

Reimer-Torn, Susan, and Nancy Reynolds. *Dance Classics.* Pennington, N.J.: Chicago Review Press, 1991.

Robbins, Jane. *Classical Dance: The Balletgoer's Guide to Technique and Performance.* New York: Holt, Rinehart and Winston, 1981.

Siegel, Beatrice. *Alicia Alonso: The Story of a Ballerina.* New York: Frederick Warne, 1979.

Simón, Pedro. *Alicia Alonso: Diálogos con la Danza.* La Habana: Editorial Letras Cubanas, 1986.

Taper, Bernard. *Balanchine: A Biography.* New York: Times Books, 1984.

Terry, Walter. *Alicia and Her Ballet Nacional de Cuba.* Garden City, N.Y.: Doubleday, 1981.

Whiehill, Angela, and William Noble. *The Young Professional's Book of Ballet.* Pennington, N.J.: Dance Horizon/Princeton Book Company, 1990.

INDEX

Alonso, Fernando, 11, 19,
20, 32, 33, 35, 36, 53,
55, 57, 58, 59, 62, 63,
69, 71, 72, 74, 76
Alicia's divorce of, 86
Alicia's marriage to, 13
as director of Ballet Alicia
Alonso, 53–54
move to New York by,
12–13
roles of, 16, 17, 18, 23–24
Alonso, Laurita, 13, 16, 20,
23, 34, 36, 59, 62–63,
68, 90
American Ballet Caravan,
19–22, 23, 24
American Ballet Theatre,
16, 24–31, 32, 33, 36,
37–52, 53, 54, 55, 58–
62, 64, 70, 72, 73, 84,
86.
American National Theater
and Academy (ANTA),
59
Apollo, 46, 61

Bach, Johann Sebastian, 36
Balanchine, George, 12–13,
19, 46, 49, 61
ballet:
Cuban school of, 63
five positions of, 14–15
Italian school of, 14–15
psycho-, 77

Ballet Alicia Alonso, 53–59,
62, 63–64, 65, 66, 71–
72
Latin American tours of,
54–57
Ballet Caravan, *see* American
Ballet Caravan
Ballet de Camagüey, 76
Ballet de Cuba, *see* Ballet
Alicia Alonso
Ballet Nacional (Budapest),
83
Ballet Nacional de Cuba,
71–78, 79, 83–84, 88,
89
Ballet Russe de Monte
Carlo, 12, 18, 19, 35,
38, 48, 64–65, 67, 68,
70, 72
Ballet Theatre, *see* American
Ballet Theatre
Barnes, Charles, 17
Baronova, Irina, 38
Barraguer, Joaquín, 83
Barzel, Ann, 61
Batista, Fulgencio, 65
Bentley, Muriel, 25, 59
Bernstein, Leonard, 38
Billy the Kid, 21, 22, 28–29,
31
Bizet, Georges, 85
Bolshoi Ballet, 68–69, 72
Broadway, 17–18, 19